AF700959

Palgrave Studies in Ancient Economies

Series Editors
Paul Erdkamp, Vrije Universiteit Brussel, Brussels, Belgium
Kenneth Hirth, Pennsylvania State University, University Park, USA
Claire Holleran, University of Exeter, Exeter, UK
Michael Jursa, University of Vienna, Vienna, Austria
Jaehwan Lee, Department of History, Chung-Ang University, Seoul, Korea (Republic of)
William Guanglin Liu, Lingnan University, Tuen Mun, Hong Kong
J. G. Manning, Yale University, New Haven, USA
Himanshu Prabha Ray, Gurugram, India

This series provides a unique dedicated forum for ancient economic historians to publish studies that make use of current theories, models, concepts, and approaches drawn from the social sciences and the discipline of economics, as well as studies that use an explicitly comparative methodology. Such theoretical and comparative approaches to the ancient economy promotes the incorporation of the ancient world into studies of economic history more broadly, ending the tradition of viewing antiquity as something separate or 'other'.

The series not only focuses on the ancient Mediterranean world, but also includes studies of ancient China, India, and the Americas pre-1500. This encourages scholars working in different regions and cultures to explore connections and comparisons between economic systems and processes, opening up dialogue and encouraging new approaches to ancient economies.

Eivind Heldaas Seland

Long-Distance Trade in the Ancient World

A Network History

palgrave
macmillan

Eivind Heldaas Seland
Department of Archeology, History,
Cultural Studies & Religion
University of Bergen
Bergen, Norway

ISSN 2752-3292 ISSN 2752-3306 (electronic)
Palgrave Studies in Ancient Economies
ISBN 978-3-031-90854-5 ISBN 978-3-031-90855-2 (eBook)
https://doi.org/10.1007/978-3-031-90855-2

© The Editor(s) (if applicable) and The Author(s), under exclusive license to Springer Nature Switzerland AG 2026

This work is subject to copyright. All rights are solely and exclusively licensed by the Publisher, whether the whole or part of the material is concerned, specifically the rights of translation, reprinting, reuse of illustrations, recitation, broadcasting, reproduction on microfilms or in any other physical way, and transmission or information storage and retrieval, electronic adaptation, computer software, or by similar or dissimilar methodology now known or hereafter developed.
The use of general descriptive names, registered names, trademarks, service marks, etc. in this publication does not imply, even in the absence of a specific statement, that such names are exempt from the relevant protective laws and regulations and therefore free for general use.
The publisher, the authors and the editors are safe to assume that the advice and information in this book are believed to be true and accurate at the date of publication. Neither the publisher nor the authors or the editors give a warranty, expressed or implied, with respect to the material contained herein or for any errors or omissions that may have been made. The publisher remains neutral with regard to jurisdictional claims in published maps and institutional affiliations.

Cover credit: © Melisa Hasan

This Palgrave Macmillan imprint is published by the registered company Springer Nature Switzerland AG
The registered company address is: Gewerbestrasse 11, 6330 Cham, Switzerland

If disposing of this product, please recycle the paper.

Competing Interests The author has no competing interests to declare that are relevant to the content of this manuscript.

Preface

This book began as a series of lectures delivered at the UrbNet Centre for Urban Network Evolutions, Aarhus University, during my tenure as a guest professor in the spring semester of 2019. I am deeply grateful to the centre's directors, Rubina Raja and Søren M. Sindbæk, for their generous invitation, and to the staff, faculty, students and fellow visitors for making my stay both memorable and intellectually rewarding. The research was supported by the Danish National Research Foundation (grant DNRF119), held by Rubina Raja.

I would also like to thank Søren M. Sindbæk, Tomáš Glomb, Francesca Mazzilli, the editors of the *Palgrave Ancient Economies* series, and the anonymous reviewers for their many helpful corrections, suggestions and constructive criticisms. I am further indebted to Jørgen Christian Meyer and Christian Julien Robin for kindly allowing me to reproduce their photographs.

While I have benefited greatly from the insights and generosity of others, all errors are mine alone.

Bergen, Norway
August 2025

Eivind Heldaas Seland

Contents

Abbreviations

Ammianus Marcellinus, *Res Gestae*, ed. Rolfe, J.C. (1956) Ammianus Marcellinus, Roman History. Harvard University Press.

Aristotle, *HN*., ed. Peck, A.L. (1965). Aristotle, *History of Animals* Harvard University Press.

Demosthenes, *Or.*, ed. Murray, A. T. (1994). *Demosthenes, Orations.* Harvard University Press.

Kosmas Indikopleustes, *Christian Topography*, ed. Wolska-Conus, W. (1968). *Cosmas Indicopleustes: Topographie Chrétienne*. Cerf.

Periplus, ed. Casson, L. (1989). *The Periplus Maris Erythraei*. Princeton University Press.

Plato, *Laws*, ed. Bury, R.G. (1926). *Plato, Laws*. Harvard University Press

Pliny, *NH*, ed. Rackham, H. (1997). Pliny, *Natural History with an English Translation by H. Rackham, W. H. S. Jones, D. E. Eichholz*. Harvard University Press.

Ptolemy, *Geography*, ed. Nobbe, C. F. A. (1843). *Claudii Ptolemaei Geographia.* Carolus Tauchnitus.

Strabo, *Geography*, ed. Jones, H. L. (2001). *The Geography of Strabo with an English Translation*. Harvard University Press.

List of Figures

CHAPTER 1

Cities, Networks, Trade and Environment

Abstract This chapter explains how the book departs from earlier studies of ancient long-distance trade in taking the academic traditions of Global history and Environmental history as its points of departure, aiming to see beyond states and empires as the dominant analytical categories, and to appreciate the role of the natural environment in enabling, shaping and restricting production, movement and exchange. The chapter then introduces three concepts that serve to integrate the narrative: cities, trade and networks. After outlining key scholarly debates on these topics within archaeology and ancient history, it is argued that the growth of urbanism, long-distance trade and connectivity were three central phenomena of Afro-Eurasian history in the so-called Long Classical Millennium (fourth century BCE to eight century CE), and that historical network theory provides tools that allow us to study them within a unified analytical framework.

Keywords Urbanism · Long-distance trade · Global history · Environmental history · Network theory · Afro-Eurasian history · Ancient economies

© The Author(s), under exclusive license to Springer Nature Switzerland AG 2026

E. H. Seland, *Long-Distance Trade in the Ancient World*, Palgrave Studies in Ancient Economies,
https://doi.org/10.1007/978-3-031-90855-2_1

Two millennia ago, in the early decades of the Common Era, the traveler and polymath Strabo was hard at work on what was to become his final project. This was nothing short of a 17 books' description of the known world, a *Geographika*. Strabo had been born in the city of Amnesia in northern Anatolia. The great event of his generation had been the transformation of the Roman republic into a principate under Augustus, the first Roman emperor, whom he outlived by a few years. Spending the last years of his exceptionally long life, he died at c. 90, in the imperial capital of Rome, Strabo had used much of his life traveling Augustus' empire. He has provided us with one of the most detailed surviving descriptions of a second ancient metropolis, Alexandria in Egypt, a city where he had lived several years as a middle-aged man. This is how he described its location:

> The greatest advantage of the city is that it is the only place in all of Egypt naturally good in both ways; that from the sea and that from the country, because the river easily carries everything that comes into this region, the greatest emporium in the inhabited world—Str. 17.1.13, transl. Roller (2014).

The passage describes how Alexandria had become the splendid city that it was, one of the greatest of the world, because of its location at the intersection of two networks, that of the Mediterranean and that of the Nile. These networks were so important because they had enabled Alexandria to become the greatest market(place) of its time. In the next paragraph Strabo also introduced the Red Sea, which to him would also include what we today call the Indian Ocean. By way of caravan roads through the eastern desert of Egypt and a canal constructed by one of the last Egyptian pharaohs and used and maintained on an off until the early Islamic period, the Red Sea connected Alexandriawith East Africa, Arabia and the wider Indian Ocean world. In this Strabo highlights three intimately related aspects of his world that he considered vital to civilized life and characteristic of his own times. These were urbanism, trade and connectivity. This small book aims to investigate how these dimensions of past societies came together in the period sometimes called the Long Classical Millennium, loosely defined from the fourth century BCE to the eight century CE (Kennedy, 2013). The ambition is to get a better understanding not only of how Strabo's world worked, but the entire ancient African-Eurasian world system, from the East China Sea to the Atlantic coast, and from the Indian Ocean to the North Sea.

Strabo clearly thought of the Augustan empire as the greatest time to be alive, and in a sense, he was warranted in his assumption that the world had never been more interconnected than in his own days. Strabo's Roman world stretched to the Syrian Desert, Arabia and Northern Mesopotamia. But in other ways his outlook was parochial, for the world was much more than Rome. To the east the Arsacid (Parthian) Empireextended to the Indus River and the Pamir Mountains. In the western Indian Ocean, maritime communities and self-confident kingdoms in present day Ethiopia, Eritrea, Yemen, Oman, Pakistan, India and Sri Lanka were competing for access to maritime networks, important trade goods and political power (Ray, 2003; Seland, 2010). In the steppes and deserts of Central and Inner Asia city states based on irrigated agriculture and long-distance trade balanced between Arsacid interest to the west and that of the Chinese Han empire (Hansen, 2015; Høisæter, 2023). In Strabo's times the interaction between these large empires and their smaller neighbors was predominantly based on peaceful trade; diplomacy and warfare playing important, but secondary roles (McLaughlin, 2010, 2014). The first century CE, however, was only one, brief, global moment in the urban system that formed, flourished and in some respects also ultimately came to decay over a span of centuries. Approaching this system as it functioned over the extended period from the mid-first millennium BCE to the late first millennium CE arguably allows us to make some general observations about the integration or lack thereof of the ancient Afroeurasian world, and the role that long-distance trade played in these processes.

A short book is obviously not sufficient to cover a millennium of world history and to do justice to a multitude of societies and communities that were all different from each other. Its claim to novelty lies in combining three approaches to history that have each had huge impact on the discipline over the last decades: Global history, Environmental history and Networked history. This book draws on material spanning from East Africa to Northern Scandinavia and from the East China Sea to the Atlantic Ocean. In terms of quantity, however, the Mediterranean, including the Roman world, West Asia and the Western Indian Ocean, receives more attention than other regions. This is likely to raise criticism, but the choice is conscious. It is made partly due to the exceptional record of data from and scholarship on these parts of the world, partly because of the role they played in connecting neighboring regions and integrating the proto-global history. Global history is not about devoting equal space to all parts of the world or about covering the history of the entire world. It is about historical narratives that transcend national and imperial boundaries and address the communalities and contingencies as well as the divergences between human societies, the connections as well as disconnections that have characterized the human past on a global or in this case proto-global scale. The Afroeurasian system of the Long Classical Millennium did not include the entire world, but in many respects it functioned as a self-contained world system to the people who inhabited it and might be studied as such (Beaujard, 2005; Crossley, 2008; Seland, 2008). Thus, case studies and examples discussed in this book are not intended to be exhaustive in their own right, but rather to be illustrative of more general trends and phenomena.

Environmental history deals with the entanglement between humans and their natural environments, including the physical world and the plants and non-human animals that inhabit it. Every aspect of ancient life depended on this natural environment in much more direct and potentially dramatic manner than most of us are used to in the modern world. In a world void of synthetic processes, all goods for consumption and trade were extracted from animals, plants, the water or the earth, and processed mainly through manual labor. Productivity, transport and availability depended directly on climatic and topographic features and on weather and seasonality. All energy came from the sun. By way of photosynthesis, it became available for animals and humans as biological energy, or in the form of winds propelling ships across the Indian Ocean and the Mediterranean Sea through the great weather systems. This dependency on highly varied geographical and climatic environments also created demand for products that originated far away. Exotic products became attractive for their visual, olfactory, gustatory, textural, medicinal or magical properties also because local alternatives simply did not exist (Purcell, 2016). This has never been a secret to scholars of ancient trade, but nevertheless, most studies have emphasized traders, trade routes, trade goods and socioeconomic frameworks over environmental conditions. These more traditional topics are also discussed in this book, but in addition, the roles of physical environments, climate, materiality and human entanglement with animals and plants are addressed.

Historians have long recognized and emphasized the difference between the past as a near infinite reservoir of agents, actions and events, most of which it is not possible to have any secure knowledge about, and the role of the historian in structuring the data that we do possess from this past into narratives about this past, that make sense in the present (Carrard, 1992; Rüsen, 2005; Veyne, 1971). The process of structuring data into narratives inevitably goes by way of our present-day assumptions about what the past was like, that is by way of theory. In this attempt to demonstrate the interconnectedness of the ancient world I draw on different strands of network theory that help lend meaning to our dispersed and fragmentary data and thus enable us to create narratives that contribute toward an integrated understanding of global or rather proto-global history in the centuries around the turn of our era. Theory, however, is means to an end, and serves here as basis for discussions of the archeological, historical and scientific evidence. Below some theoretical approaches to cities, networks and trade are outlined. In combination they allow for the third main approach in this book, that of Networked history.

Cities

The mid-first millennium BCE constitutes a global breakthrough for urbanism, cities increasingly and over time appearing in large numbers in a belt between c. 20 and c. 50 degrees northern latitude (Chandler, 1987; Modelski, 2003). These are mostly subtropical and temperate climates with sufficient areas of soil and topographies suitable for the cultivation of cereals, including rice and maize, to provide the surplus of carbohydrates necessary to support large urban populations. It might be argued that even though urbanism develops into a global phenomenon, using cities as the main category of analysis is exclusionary (Scott, 2017, pp. 13–15). Even today, according to World Bank data, no more than 58% of world population lives in cities (World Bank, 2025). In the Roman empire in the days of Strabo it might have been 10–15% of a population of 50–75 millions, that again being c. 25% of a world population roughly estimated at 225.8 million people at the turn of the common era (Maddison, 2001; Scheidel, 2004; Wilson, 2011, pp. 193–195). Outside the Mediterranean world and parts of Mesopotamia and East Asia, this segment was likely smaller. This, however, is arguably an argument in favor of studying cities as parts of networks rather than by themselves, as is attempted here, as networks integrate cities with their rural hinterlands, some close by, others widely dispersed (Hanson, 2016, pp. 18–19; Horden & Purcell, 2000, pp. 115–122).

Scholars have struggled to find good definitions of the city (De Ligt & Bintliff, 2019, pp. 9–15; Hanson, 2016, pp. 18–24; Smith, 2016; Zuiderhoek, 2016, pp. 4–9). Cities in the Mediterranean were very different from those found in Central Europe, East Africa, Arabia, India, Central Asia and East Asia at the same time. Some definitions exclude settlements that have too few inhabitants, too low density or too large seasonal variations to satisfy some arbitrary criterium but nevertheless filled many of the functions that cities do. Other settlements, while quite large and densely populated, fail to display the diversity in livelihood and demographics, all-year occupation and central functions that modern scholars expect from cities (Horden & Purcell, 2000, pp. 96–98; Weber, 1999, pp. 59–100). For urban historians and archaeologists definitions lack flexibility and are arguably of limited use as they might exclude places that have relevance to the problems we want to investigate (Smith, 2016, p. 166). If an understanding of what the ancient city was is nevertheless called for, a functional definition along the lines of that offered by Bruce Trigger as "a unit of settlement which performs specialized functions in relationship to a broad hinterland" might do for the purposes of this book, in which the city is not studied for its own sake, but as a part of wider networks (Smith, 2016, p. 154; Trigger, 1972, p. 577). This approach is inspired by Walter Christaller's work on cities and other locations as 'Central Places', that offer a range of services or functions to their hinterlands (Bekker-Nielsen, 2020, pp. 84–86; Christaller, 1933). Some functions, such as a weekly market, would be available in many places, while others, like a court of law, a religious festival or a long-distance trading fair might only be present in centers of higher centrality and at longer intervals (Bekker-Nielsen, 1989, 2020; De Ligt, 1993; Hanson, 2016, p. 30). With regard to long-distance trade such functions discussed in more detail in this book include, but are not limited to production, protection, conflict resolution, taxation, exchange and transport.

As for types of cities, urban history as a discipline was profoundly shaped by German sociologist Max Weber, who in his famous essay, *The City*, published just over a century ago, made an economic distinction between consumer- and production cities (Weber, 1999, pp. 59–67). Weber, before becoming one of the founding fathers of modern sociology, had started his academic life as a historian of Roman law and economy. Drawing on the work of Werner Sombart (1902, pp. 196–205) he held that most cities of the ancient world, the prime example of course being Rome, to be 'consumer cities', dominated by land-owning elites, who consumed the products of urban hinterlands. This surplus they channeled in their own direction through taxes, tribute and rent. In contrast to this Weber saw the Medieval and Early Modern 'production city,' where artisans and merchants created the economic basis for the urban settlement by producing and exchanging manufactured goods. Urban studies have moved far in the century since Weber, but his models are still cited because they remain useful and have the advantage of being intuitive and easily applicable. Weber understood that all real cities would display a range of economic activities and that his models were ideal types. Three brief observations, however, relate his typology with the two other main topics of this study, trade and networks. The first it that consumption as well as production largely depends on exchange. The elites of consumer cities would also attract traders and artisans through their consumption of their landed wealth. This is true to some extent even when dealing with non-market mechanisms such as taxes and rents, and for Weber trade was a basic defining trait of any form of urbanism (North, 1977; Seland, 2022; Weber, 1999, pp. 61–62). The second observation is that consumption as well as production depend on and describe the existence of networks integrating cities with their economic and social hinterlands. The third point is that Weber also operated with the less famous ideal type of 'the merchant city,' which was a settlement specialized in the role of mediator between other cities, that he believed had been less common, but nevertheless in existence both in the ancient and in the medieval/early modern periods (Weber, 1999, pp. 65–66). In archaeology and premodern history Karl Polanyi's model of the port of trade, a small, autonomous polity, typically a city situated on the edge of a larger territorial state and at the interface between communication networks such as oceans, deserts or rivers, gained some traction, but also quite a bit of notoriety, due to Polanyi's insistence that price-setting markets did not exist in the ancient world (Manning, 2018, pp. 9–13; Polanyi, 1963; Seland, 2017). A more inclusive ideal type or model allowing both for market trade and non-commercial relationships between city and hinterland is that of the gateway city, proposed by urban geographer Andrew Burghardt (1971). Burghard, who studied nineteenth- and twentieth-century urbanization, was interested in the role of cities in integrating distinct networks. His case studies were cities established on the edges of the North American Great Plains and along Eastern European railway networks in the nineteenth century. These not only served as central places in providing services to their rural hinterlands but had the additional function of providing access to resources from economically different networks. In studies of the ancient world, Burghard's model has been used on communities situated between empires and between ecologically determined communication and subsistence networks such as oceans and deserts (Seland, 2021; Sommer, 2018). As we shall see below, cities frequently served as gateways or bottlenecks, facilitating and regulating, and by that also restricting the movement of goods and people between regional networks otherwise defined by political borders or ecological constraints. This could for instance be because inter-polity trade was restricted by law to certain markets or because the interplay between geography and society demanded a change of transport regime or a seasonal break before movement could recommence. Alexandria as described by Strabo was such a gateway city, integrating the ecologically shaped communication networks of Egypt, the Mediterranean and the Red Sea, to say nothing of the diverse social networks of Egypt, the Mediterranean and the African hinterland. Other gateway cities existed at the intersection of other such communication networks across the Afroeurasian world.

Trade and Exchange

Urbanism became a global phenomenon within the Afro-Eurasian system in the Long Classical Millennium. Each city belonged in its own local and regional context and came into existence for specific reasons that are sometimes known, more often not. Still, a development that took place on global, i.e., system-wide scale, should also be seen in context with other developments on that level. The belt of cities across subtropical and temperate climate zones in the northern hemisphere benefitted from the benign and stable climate of the late centuries BCE and the early centuries CE known as the Roman Climate Optimum (RCO), which despite its name was a global phenomenon. Warmer temperatures than those of preceding and subsequent periods extended growing seasons in areas of high altitude and latitude and boosted the great weather systems, the pacific ENSO (El Niño Southern Oscillation), the Indian Ocean monsoons and the NAO (North Atlantic Oscillation) that brought precipitation to the Afroeurasian landmass. Extreme weather events still happened, but judging from scientific and historical records less often than in the preceding and following periods (Ljungqvist, 2017, pp. 111–125; McCormick, 2013; Scheidel, 2018). Favorable and stable climate must have facilitated urbanism through increased and more predictable food supply, in turn enabling population growth and urban life (Harper, 2017, pp. 23–64; Issar & Zohar, 2007, pp. 193–220; Ljungqvist, 2017, pp. 111–125).

Urbanism was also facilitated by and in many cases initiated as part of processes of state and empire formation that played out on a proto-global level in Eurasia and North Africa in this period, spanning from Qin- and Han-China to successive Indian, Persianate, Hellenistic empires and the Roman empire (Bang et al., 2020). Trade, or better "exchange," which covers a wider set of mechanisms by which resources changed hand, is a third system-wide phenomenon that developed along the same geographical axes as cities. Trade routes, on land as well as on water, spanned from the Atlantic to the East China Sea and from the North Sea and Baltic to the Indian Ocean and across the Sahara. They transcended urbanized regions, bringing the world of cities into contact with the non-urban world.

Few aspects of ancient history have caused more debates with less fruitful results than the role of trade in ancient economies. Through much of the twentieth-century scholars heatedly debated whether ancient economies were primarily consumption, subsistence and status oriented, trade and markets playing subordinate roles to social institutions in the distribution of wealth, or whether ancient economies simply represented less developed versions of modern market economies (cf. Horden & Purcell, 2000, pp. 123–172; Manning, 2018, pp. 17–71; Seland, 2017). With the advantage of hindsight, the minimalist side clearly ascribed too little importance to price-setting markets in the ancient world. The maximalist side, however, was also mistaken in turning a blind eye to the fact that resources also change hand by a number of institutions other than market trade, and that this remains so even today (Granovetter, 1985). One scholar who recognized this early was Douglass C. North (North, 1977). North became one of the pioneers of the school known as New Institutional Economics (NIE), which study the influence of institutions on economic performance. Over time North developed a framework for historical analysis where he described the world in terms of what he called organizations and institutions (North, 1990; North et al., 2009). By organizations he referred to "groups of people pursuing a mix of individual ***and*** common goals through partially coordinated behaviour" (North et al., 2009, p. 15). Examples could be a modern sports club, a state, a merchant association, a robber band or a nomadic tribe. Institutions he famously described as 'the rules of the game,' being the patterns of interaction between groups as well as between individual agents (North et al., 2009, p. 15). Institutions could be anything from traditions of gift-giving and dowries, through market trade and taxes, to the custom of letting soldiers pillage a conquered city, but leaving one that surrendered intact. North described premodern societies as dominated by political organizations, that is organizations specialized in the use and containment of violence. These would invariably act in a rent-seeking manner, using their capacity for violence to direct a maximum of resources toward themselves, for instance through war, tribute, and extortion, but also through protecting and taxing trade and production whenever that was in their interest, because it might limit expensive use of force and increase the return by not killing the proverbial goose that lays the golden egg (North et al., 2009, pp. 30–54).

North's approach, along with others from the field of NIE, have served to revitalize scholarship on ancient economies over the last decades allowing the study of all kinds of economic interaction within the same framework and underlining that economic interaction is also social interaction and thus takes place within social networks (Bang, 2007, 2008; Droß-Krüpe et al., 2016; Scheidel et al., 2007). Indeed, organizations in the sense of North *are* social networks and institutions are the ties or edges that interconnect them. For the present purpose the approach has the advantage of opening the perspective also of cities being organizations and thus social networks in their own right, on par with states, merchant associations and ethnic groups.

Networks

> No man is an island entire of itself; every man is a piece of the continent, a part of the main—John Donne (1624)

The insight that the world is interconnected and that changes in one part of a system will invariably affect the other parts is by no means new, as these famous lines signify. While beautifully expressed by Donne this was no original thought in his age, but deeply ingrained in ancient and medieval political theory (Martins, 2019). Scholars of the past have with good reason been skeptical of diffusionist narratives considering the strong role played by history and archaeology in legitimizing modern imperialism (see, e.g., Gosden, 2004; Ray, 2008). But in recent decades network approaches to history and archaeology have arguably made it possible to move past old notions of center and periphery or imperialism and response in the study of how long-distance interaction shaped premodern societies. Social scientists have been interested in social networks at least since the 1930s (Wasserman & Faust, 1994, pp. 10–17). Early hallmark studies include Stanley Milgram's six degrees of separation experiment, demonstrating and popularizing the validity of Donne's poetic observation by showing how most Americans of his time were indirectly connected with each other through a limited number of intermediaries (Milgram, 1967). Mark Granovetter's study of the American labor market resulted in his famous "Strength of weak ties" theory, showing the potential of open access networks based on casual connections in disseminating information (Granovetter, 1973). Advances in graph science and statistics gradually made software and methodologies accessible to a broad community of scholars in the toolset that goes under the shorthands of Social Network Analysis and Network Science (Wasserman & Faust, 1994). This tradition was occasionally drawn upon in archaeology and history since the 1970s, but had its breakthrough in the 2010s, network analysis becoming a standard tool of the trade, especially to archaeologists,reinvigorating a discipline in search of firm ground (Brughmans, 2010, 2012; Collar et al., 2015; Knappett, 2013; Mills, 2017).

The popularity of formal and quantitative approaches had been anticipated by theoretical work of social scientist in the 1980s and 1990s, allowing historians and archaeologists to use network thinking as heuristic tools (Knappett, 2016). As noted above, NIE uses social networks to explain why the market-centered approaches of neo-classical economics failed to adequately explain economic behavior in many cases where social relations influence the allocation of resources (Landa, 1994; North, 1990; North et al., 2009; Wickström & Landa, 2018). Manuel Castell's theory of the Network Society described a world where access to knowledge- and information networks determined who would be winners and losers just at the time when the Internet started to become relevant to ordinary people (Castells, 1996). Historical sociologist Michael Mann's theory of power explained how this manifests itself in social networks rather than in institutions or actors, as power is always exercised by someone in relation to someone. Mann identified ideology, economy, military capacity and politics as the four sources of such social power, hence his model is known as IEMP (Mann, 1986). Bruno Latour's work on Actor-Networks, where he insisted that objects and the physical world serve as what he calls actants, instrumental in generating and maintaining networks also between living beings, has become fundamental for archaeology in creating a bridge between social worlds and material surroundings and for the study of human environment entanglement (Hodder, 2012; Latour, 1993, 2005). Together these approaches amount to what can be characterized as nothing short of a 'relational turn' in the social sciences and humanities, building on and supplementing the linguistic, spatial and material turns that have already shaped scholarship since the 1970 (Brughmans et al., 2016, p. 7; Teigen & Seland, 2017). The combination of formal and qualitative approaches, providing visualization and testability along with explanative potential have, however, proven fruitful, providing novel insights into a number of aspects of ancient societies (Collar, 2013; Malkin, 2011; Schor, 2011).

Structure of This Book

The relational turn that brought networks and connectivity (back) into history without the traditional hierarchy between center and periphery is by far not the only major change to how we approach and conceive of the ancient world that has taken place over recent decades. Of equal importance was the material turn that emphasized how our physical surroundings fundamentally and directly shape and influence how we live, think and act, and in that sense takes on agency of its own (Hodder, 2012; Latour, 1993, 2005). Related was also the spatial turn, that emphasized how our lives play out in geographical and social space (Fletcher, 2004, 2010; Soja, 1996). Students of premodern history have long been interested in how geographical space contained and enabled cultural, social, commercial and political interaction (Braudel, 1966; Broodbank, 2015; Horden & Purcell, 2000; Wick, 2016). Recent scholarship in the classical disciplines also increasingly emphasize how sociopolitical developments were directly influenced by factors such as climate change, energy consumption and microbiological dynamics (Harper, 2017; Woolf, 2020). New archaeological data shedding light on ancient connectivity increasingly stem from bioarcheological research (e.g., Boivin et al., 2012;

Cappers, 2006). In sum scholars have increasingly come to see past societies in context of how they engaged also with their non-human surroundings. These developments all point toward the importance of the natural environment also for phenomena such as urbanism and trade, that long used to be the preserve of social scientists. Taking this cue, this book integrates landscapes, oceans, climate, flora and fauna in its narrative of ancient world trade. Without downplaying the importance of merchants, markets, ships and roads, it also describes how production and transport were shaped by seasonality, weather regimes and pack animals; and how human and non-human agents such as microorganisms, plants and animals interacted in networks that were both social and tangible at the same time. Inspired by the paradigm of structural history that many pioneers of environmental history worked within (cf. Carrard, 1992), it contains no chronological narrative, but approaches its topic from a series of angles that highlight different aspects of the networks that came to interconnect the world of the Long Classical Millennium.

In summary, cities are an important topic of history because their growth and spread are among the most prominent phenomena in the period we are studying and among the most lasting historical legacies from the ancient world. Cities should be investigated in conjunction with exchange, as trade was the only anthropogenic agent of change that operated on a system-wide, proto-global scale within the urban networks of this period. Cities and trade both lend themselves easily to network approaches and can indeed be studies as networks in their own right. Network theory and analysis provide the tools needed in order to address cities and trade within the same framework and thus understand their relationship. The next chapter will address cities as parts of networks of places, before looking at how they also became integrated in networks of things (Chapter 3), people (Chapter 4) and animals (Chapter 5), before these elements are brought together in a discussion of the spatiality of ancient world trade (Chapter 6) (Fig. 1.1).

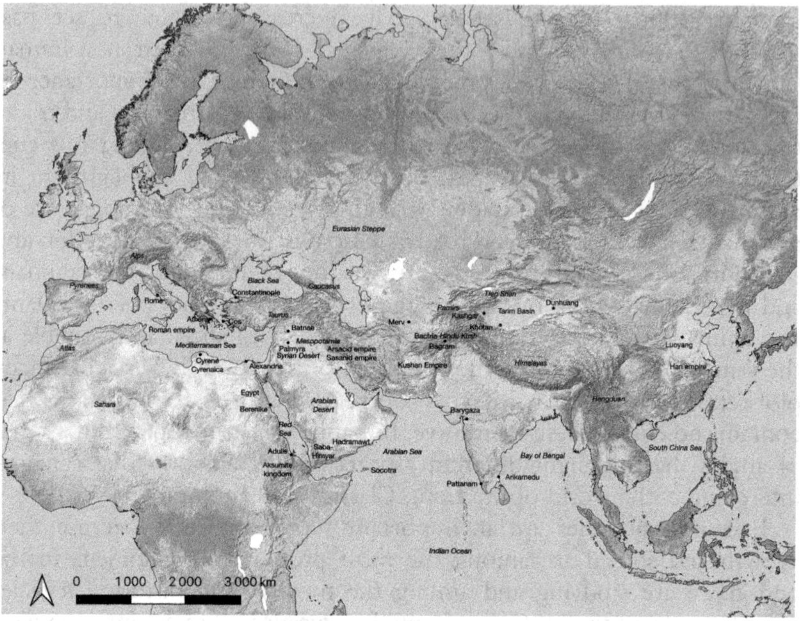

Fig. 1.1 Map of important places, features and polities mentioned in the text. Basemap U.S. National Park Service. Public Domain

References

Bang, P. F. (2007). Trade and empire—In search of organizing concepts for the Roman economy. *Past and Present, 195*, 3–54.

Bang, P. F. (2008). *The Roman bazaar: A comparative study of trade and markets in a tributary empire*. Cambridge University Press.

Bang, P. F., Bayly, C. A., & Scheidel, W. (Eds.). (2020). *The Oxford world history of empire: Volume two: The history of empires*. Oxford University Press.

Beaujard, P. (2005). The Indian Ocean in Eurasian and African world-systems before the sixteenth century. *Journal of World History, 16*, 411–465.

Bekker-Nielsen, T. (1989). *The geography of power: Studies in the urbanization of Roman North-West Europe*. B.A.R.

Bekker-Nielsen, T. (2020). The Roman city as a central place. In I. B. Mæhle, P. B. Ravnå, & E. H. Seland (Eds.), *Methods and models in ancient history. Studies in honor of Jørgen Christian Meyer* (pp. 81–98). Norwegian Institute at Athens.

Boivin, N., Fuller, D. Q., & Crowther, A. (2012). Old World globalization and the Columbian exchange: Comparison and contrast. *World Archaeology, 44*, 452–469.

Braudel, F. (1966). *La Méditerranée et le monde méditerranéen à l'époque de Philippe II*. A. Colin.

Broodbank, C. (2015). *The making of the Middle Sea: A history of the Mediterranean from the beginning to the emergence of the classical world*. Thames & Hudson.

Brughmans, T. (2010). Connecting the dots: Towards archaeological network analysis. *Oxford Journal of Archaeology, 29*(3), 277–303.

Brughmans, T. (2012). Thinking through networks: A review of formal network methods in archaeology. *Journal of Archaeological Method and Theory, 20*, 623–662.

Brughmans, T., Collar, A., & Coward, F. (2016). *The connected past: Challenges to network studies in archaeology and history*. Oxford University Press.

Burghardt, A. F. (1971). A hypothesis about gateway cities. *Annals of the Association of American Geographers, 61*(2), 269–285.

Cappers, R. T. J. (2006). *Roman foodprints at Berenike: Archaeobotanical evidence of subsistence and trade in the Eastern desert of Egypt*. University of California Los Angeles.

Carrard, P. (1992). *Poetics of the new history: French historical discourse from Braudel to Chartier*. Johns Hopkins University Press.

Castells, M. (1996). *The information age: Economy, society and culture: Vol. 1: The rise of the network society*. Blackwell.

Chandler, T. (1987). *Four thousand years of urban growth: An historical census*. St. David's University Press.

Christaller, W. (1933). *Die zentralen Orte in Süddeutschland: Eine ökonomisch-geographische Untersuchung über die Gesetzmässigkeit der Verbreitung und Entwicklung der Siedlungen mit städtischen Funktionen*. Verlag von Gustav Fischer.

Collar, A. (2013). *Religious networks in the Roman Empire: The spread of new ideas*. Cambridge University Press.

Collar, A., Coward, F., Brughmans, T., & Mills, B. (2015). Networks in archaeology: Phenomena, abstraction, representation. *Journal of Archaeological Method and Theory, 22*(1), 1–32.

Crossley, P. K. (2008). *What is global history?* Polity Press.

De Ligt, L. (1993). *Fairs and markets in the Roman Empire: Economic and social aspects of periodic trade in a pre-industrial society*. Brill.

De Ligt, L., & Bintliff, J. (2019). *Regional urban systems in the Roman world, 150 BCE–250 CE*. Brill.

Droß-Krüpe, K., Ruffing, K., & Föllinger, S. (2016). *Antike Wirtschaft und ihre kulturelle Prägung*. Harrassowitz Verlag.

Fletcher, R. (2004). Materiality, space, time, and outcome. In J. Bintliff (Ed.), *A companion to archaeology* (pp. 110–140). Blackwell.
Fletcher, R. (2010). Urban materialities: Meaning, magnitude, friction, and outcomes. In D. Hicks (Ed.), *The Oxford handbook of material culture studies* (pp. 459–483). Oxford University Press.
Gosden, C. (2004). *Archaeology and colonialism: Cultural contact from 5000 B.C. to the present*. Cambridge University Press.
Granovetter, M. S. (1973). The strength of weak ties. *American Journal of Sociology, 78*(6), 1360–1380.
Granovetter, M. S. (1985). Economic action and social structure: The problem of embeddedness. *American Journal of Sociology, 91*(3), 481–510.
Hansen, V. (2015). *The Silk Road: A new history*. Oxford University Press.
Hanson, J. W. (2016). *An urban geography of the Roman world, 100 BC to AD 300*. Archaeopress Publishing Ltd.
Harper, K. (2017). *The fate of Rome: Climate, disease, and the end of an empire*. Princeton University Press.
Hodder, I. (2012). *Entangled: An archaeology of the relationships between humans and things*. Wiley-Blackwell.
Horden, P., & Purcell, N. (2000). *The corrupting sea: A study of Mediterranean history*. Blackwell.
Høisæter, T. L. (2023). Islands in a sea of sand: The role of Tarim Basin polities in global trade during late antiquity. *Journal of Global History, 18*(3), 401–425.
Issar, A. S., & Zohar, M. (2007). *Climate change: Environment and history of the near east*. Springer.
Kennedy, D. (2013). *Gerasa and the Decapolis*. Bloomsbury Publishing.
Knappett, C. (2013). *Network analysis in archaeology: New approaches to regional interaction*. Oxford University Press.
Knappett, C. (2016). Networks in archaeology: Between scientific method and humanistic metaphor. In T. Brughmans, A. Collar, & F. Coward (Eds.), *The connected past: Challenges to network studies in archaeology and history* (pp. 21–33). Oxford University Press.
Landa, J. T. (1994). *Trust, ethnicity, and identity: Beyond the new institutional economics of ethnic trading networks, contract law, and gift-exchange*. University of Michigan Press.
Latour, B. (1993). *We have never been modern*. Harvester Wheatsheaf.
Latour, B. (2005). *Reassembling the social—An introduction to actor-network-theory*. Oxford University Press.
Ljungqvist, F. C. (2017). *Klimatet och människan under 12000 år*. Dialogos.
Maddison, A. (2001). *The world economy: A millennial perspective*. OECD Publishing.

Malkin, I. (2011). *A small Greek world: Networks in the ancient Mediterranean*. Oxford University Press.

Mann, M. (1986). *The sources of social power*. Cambridge University Press.

Manning, J. G. (2018). *The open sea: The economic life of the ancient Mediterranean world from the Iron Age to the rise of Rome*. Princeton University Press.

Martins, A. R. (2019). The zoon politikon: Medieval Aristotelian interpretations. *Revista Portuguesa De Filosofia, 75*(3), 1539–1574.

McCormick, M. (2013). Geodatabase of historical evidence on Roman and post-Roman climate. *Harvard Dataverse*, V4.

McLaughlin, R. (2010). *Rome and the distant East: Trade routes to the ancient lands of Arabia, India and China*. Continuum.

McLaughlin, R. (2014). *The Roman Empire and the Indian Ocean: The ancient world economy and the kingdoms of Africa, Arabia and India*. Pen & Sword Books.

Milgram, S. (1967). Six degrees of separation. *Psychology Today, 2*, 60–64.

Mills, B. J. (2017). Social network analysis in archaeology. *Annual Review of Anthropology, 46*, 379–397.

Modelski, G. (2003). *World cities: -3000 to 2000*. Faros 2000.

North, D. C. (1977). Markets and other allocation systems in history: The challenge of Karl Polanyi. *Journal of European Economic History, 6*(3), 703–716.

North, D. C. (1990). *Institutions, institutional change and economic performance*. Cambridge University Press.

North, D. C., Wallis, J. J., & Weingast, B. R. (2009). *Violence and social orders: A conceptual framework for interpreting recorded human history*. Cambridge University Press.

Polanyi, K. (1963). Ports of trade in early societies. *The Journal of Economic History, 23*(1), 30–45.

Purcell, N. (2016). Unnecessary dependences: Illustrating circulation in pre-modern large-scale history. In J. Belich, J. Darwin, M. Frenz, & C. Wickham (Eds.), *The prospect of global history* (pp. 65–79). Oxford University Press.

Ray, H. P. (2003). *The archaeology of seafaring in ancient South Asia*. Cambridge University Press.

Ray, H. P. (2008). *Colonial archaeology in South Asia: The legacy of Sir Mortimer Wheeler*. Oxford University Press.

Roller, D. W. (2014). *The geography of Strabo*. Cambridge University Press.

Rüsen, J. (2005). *History: Narration, interpretation, orientation*. Berghahn Books.

Scheidel, W. (2004). Demographic and economic development in the ancient Mediterranean world. *Journal of Institutional and Theoretical Economics, 160*(4), 743–757.

Scheidel, W. (2018). *The science of Roman history: Biology, climate, and the future of the past*. Princeton University Press.
Scheidel, W., Morris, I., & Saller, R. P. (2007). *The Cambridge economic history of the Greco-Roman world*. Cambridge University Press.
Schor, A. M. (2011). *Theodoret's people: Social networks and religious conflict in late Roman Syria*. University of California Press.
Scott, J. C. (2017). *Against the grain: A deep history of the earliest states*. Yale University Press.
Seland, E. H. (2008). The Indian Ocean and the globalisation of the ancient world. *Ancient West and East, 7*, 67–79.
Seland, E. H. (2010). *Ports and power in the Periplus: Complex societies and maritime trade on the Indian Ocean in the first century AD*. Archaeopress.
Seland, E. H. (2017). Approaching trade in pre-state and early state societies. In Z. T. Glørstad & K. Loftsgarden (Eds.), *Viking-Age transformations: Trade, craft and resources in Western Scandinavia* (pp. 31–41). Routledge.
Seland, E. H. (2021). Trade, traders, and religion in gateway-cities of the Roman East. *Religion in the Roman Empire (RRE), 7*(2), 297–312.
Seland, E. H. (2022). Markets in the Erythra Thalassa. In K. Dross-Krüpe & K. Ruffing (Eds.), *Markt, Märkte und Marktgebäude in der antiken Welt* (pp. 393–402). Harrassowitz.
Smith, M. E. (2016). How can archaeologists identify early cities? Definitions, types, and attributes. In *Eurasia at the dawn of history: Urbanization and social change* (pp. 153–168). Cambridge University Press.
Soja, E. W. (1996). *Thirdspace: Journeys to Los Angeles and other real-and-imagined places*. Blackwell.
Sombart, W. (1902). *Der moderne Kapitalismus 2*. Duncker & Humblot.
Sommer, M. (2018). *Roms orientalische Steppengrenze: Palmyra, Edessa, Dura-Europos, Hatra: Eine Kulturgeschichte von Pompeius bis Diocletian*. Franz Steiner.
Teigen, H. F., & Seland, E. H. (2017). Sinews of empire and the relational turn in classical scholarship. In H. F. Teigen & E. H. Seland (Eds.), *Sinews of empire: Networks in the Roman near East and beyond* (pp. v–xii). Oxbow Books.
Trigger, B. G. (1972). Determinants of urban growth in pre-industrial societies. In R. Ucko, G. Tringham, & G. W. Dimbleby (Eds.), *Man, settlement, and urbanism* (pp. 575–599). Schenkman.
Veyne, P. (1971). *Comment on ecrit l'histoire: Essai d'epistemologie*. Du Seuil.
Wasserman, S., & Faust, K. (1994). *Social network analysis: Methods and applications*. Cambridge University Press.
Weber, M. (1999). *Wirtschaft und Gesellschaft*. Mohr.
Wick, A. (2016). *The Red Sea: In search of lost space*. University of California Press.

Wickström, B.-A., & Landa, J. T. (2018). Interethnic relations, informal trading networks, and social integration: Imitation, habits, and social evolution. *Journal of Bioeconomics, 20*(3), 263–286.

Wilson, A. (2011). City sizes and urbanization in the Roman Empire. In A. K. Bowman & A. Wilson (Eds.), *Settlement, urbanization, and population* (pp. 161–195). Oxford University Press.

Woolf, G. (2020). *The life and death of ancient cities: A natural history*. Oxford University Press.

World Bank. (2025). *Urban population (% of total population)*. https://data.worldbank.org/indicator/SP.URB.TOTL.IN.ZS. Accessed July 30, 2025.

Zuiderhoek, A. (2016). *The ancient city*. Cambridge University Press.

CHAPTER 2

Places

Abstract Starting with the example of an inscription left by a visitor in a cave on the Indian Ocean island of Socotra in 258 CE, the chapter traces the steps of his journey from his native city of Palmyra, Syria. Underlining how transport and exchange of high value, low weight commodities was a main motivation for undertaking long journeys in the ancient world, and how environmental differences created demand for such products, the chapter goes on to discuss the role of topography and climate in shaping long-distance connectivity into macroregional circuits of exchange. These circuits, however, were in turn made up by agglomerations of places and microregions. Taking one of these, Cyrenaica in present-day Libya, as a first example, it is argued that each microregion can be conceived as a network cluster, connected to the overall structure through gateway settlements. The next example is the western Indian Ocean/Arabian Sea, where dispersed hinterland regions were connected by coastal and trans-oceanic contacts into a small-world network structure. The example of movement of commodities between South Asia, Central Asia and East Asia is then used to show how series of such networks integrated the Afro-Eurasian world, but that the friction caused by seasonality affecting harvest times and movement served to reinforce the role of cities placed at the intersection of regional networks as places of exchange.

© The Author(s), under exclusive license to Springer Nature Switzerland AG 2026

E. H. Seland, *Long-Distance Trade in the Ancient World*, Palgrave Studies in Ancient Economies,
https://doi.org/10.1007/978-3-031-90855-2_2

Keywords Seasonality · Connectivity · Small-world networks · Gateway settlements · Trade networks

In July of the year 258 CE a man named Abgar found himself on the island of Socotra, straight west of Cape Guardafui, the easternmost point of Africa. Proceeding almost a kilometer into a limestone cavern with only the light of torches or oil-lamps, Abgar left a message asking for the blessing of the gods of the cave. The small wooden panel remained undisturbed for some 1743 years before it was found by a team of speleologists in 2001, along with more than 200 other texts. These were for the most part in scripts that correspond to those used Gujarat and the Decan regions in western India in the third and fourth centuries of the Common Era, but also in Ancient South Arabic, Ethiopic Geʿez, Greek, and in this single instance, the variety of Aramaic script used only by the inhabitants of the Syrian city of Palmyra (Gorea, 2012; Strauch, 2012). Most are very short inscriptions in rock, likely made in gratitude for or in anticipation of safe passage. The texts give names, and in some cases, they add information on *varṇa* (caste). A handful of inscriptions also reveal professions, including captain (*nāvika*), pilot (*niryāmaka*) and possibly merchant (*vani*). Place names include Bharukaccha (modern Bharuch), which is the Barygaza of the first century CE *Periplus Maris Erythraei* (41–49) and Ptolemy's second century CE *Geography* (7.1), and Hastavapra, today the small town of Hāthab, near modern Bhavnagar in Gujarat. A few texts contain the ethnonyms *Yavana* and *Saka*. Yavana means Greek, and entered Indic languages by way of the Persian world, but is not to be taken literally at this late date, but rather, according to Strauch, pointing to erstwhile Indo-Greek regions in northwestern India. Saka refers to the kingdom of the Kṣatrapas or Western Satraps, who controlled the region around Barygaza through most of this period (Strauch, 2012, pp. 343–350) (Fig. 2.1).

Abgar was far from home. Palmyra was an oasis-city in the northern Syrian Desert, that made a fortune from operating caravans between the Arsacid and Roman empires in the first two centuries CE, and that briefly rose to geopolitical importance by taking advantage of the turmoil in the Roman empire during the mid-third century CE, and the power vacuum left by the defeat and capture of the Roman emperor Valerian on hands of his Sasanid rival, Shapur II in 260 CE (Hartmann, 2024;

Fig. 2.1 Abgar's text, "Tablet De Geest." (Photo courtesy of Christian Julien Robin. CC BY 4.0 SA)

Seland, 2016a). In order to be present at Socotra at the time and date given on the tablet, Abgar must have left his native city of Palmyra in the northern Syrian Desert at least a year earlier, and he was looking forward to a stay of no less than six months on the remote Indian Ocean island, before he would be able to return home. Socotra lacks sheltered natural harbors and remained all but isolated during the strong winds of the summer monsoon until the construction of an airport in 1999 (Van Rensburg, 2016). Over the course of his journey Abgar will likely have traveled by camel across the Syrian Desert, by riverboat or raft down the Mesopotamian rivers, and then by ship, and he will have stayed in cities in Middle and Southern Mesopotamia, Northwestern India or Southeastern Arabia, and/or Egypt, Jordan and Yemen, in order to change means of transport and arrange with passage for the next leg of his journey when the season was right. Whether he decided to return home by way of the Red Sea or the Persian Gulf, his total journey would amount to ca 10.000 kilometers if he ever saw the palm groves of his native Palmyra again (Seland, 2011, 2016a, pp. 45–61). Many of us tend to see travel as exciting and relaxing at the same time. For Abgar it was surely exciting at times, sometimes probably well across the border to frightening, but for most of the time it was likely monotonous, hard, dirty and boring. His 10.000 kilometers of adventure would be spent walking on his own sandal clad feet in temperatures between 30 and 40 °C through dusty and monotonous desert landscapes, subsiding mostly on dates, unleavened bread, water tasting of the goat skins it had been carried in, and the occasional hunted hare or gazelle. He will have navigated rafts made of floating skins, branches and twigs down the Euphrates, never more than a few inches away from the water, and spent weeks on end on the rolling and unprotected deck of a ship without a single straight surface, under the burning sun of the Arabian Sea. Chances are he would find some months of forced stay on a serene island in the Indian Ocean quite relaxing. Visiting the cave sanctuary at Hoq, Socotra, he was able to tap into networks that connected him with his home, but also with seafarers and merchants from other parts of the Indian Ocean world.

Although people in the ancient world moved for all kinds of purposes, including nomadism, transhumance, military conquest, work, slavery, pilgrimage, missionary zeal, and even tourism and wish for adventure (Casson, 1994), the long-distance mobility experts were people like Abgar—merchants. They moved because it was a way to make a living and in some cases an opportunity to get rich fast, in which case you might continue to make money, through investment in trading ventures carried out by others, without the invariably uncomfortable and sometimes dangerous traveling. Due to the prohibitive transaction and transport costs involved, trade was mostly based on high-value, durable commodities of limited availability: Silk was mainly available in China, cotton, gemstones and spices in India, frankincense and other aromatics in Arabia and the Horn of Africa, silver from the Iberian peninsula and so on. This remains true even if crops and technology moved along the trade routes over time, so that sericulture traveled from China to India and the Mediterranean by way of Central Asia and cotton was introduced to Egypt, as a result of the networks discussed in this book (Hildebrandt, 2017; Wild et al., 2008). As pointed out above, the ancient world did not know synthetic processes, and all commodities in ancient trade were animal-, plant- or rock/mineral-products. The availability of resources in any given location was determined by climate and geography. Possibilities for replacing products with substitutes were limited, and alternatives were likely to be inferior to the original quality, as for instance Pliny testifies to in his encyclopedic first century CE *Natural History* (12.32), where he discusses different varieties of, and attempts at forging and adulterating frankincense and other kinds of aromatics. Virtually all available energy came from the sun, either directly through photosynthesis, or indirectly through the consumption of biomass created by photosynthesis by animals or people (Braudel, 1981, pp. 70–91). In sum this means that climate and environment determined the limits of the possible with regard to communication, travel and trade to a much larger extent than today. This chapter addresses how this was reflected in the geographical layout and structure of ancient exchange networks.

Climate, Geography and Networks

As mentioned in the previous chapter, cities in the Long Classical Millennium were concentrated in the subtropical and temperate climate zones of the northern hemisphere, and with some notable exceptions based on irrigation, in regions that received sufficient rainfall for dry agriculture. In western Eurasia and Northern Africa the most important weather system is known as the North Atlantic Oscillation (NAO), which is a system consisting of high pressure near the Azores and a low pressure near Iceland that propels wind and moisture from the Atlantic toward Europe. In a normal winter, when the pressure difference is low, these westerlies continue southwest into the Mediterranean and provide winter rains all the way eastwards to Afghanistan, creating the possibilities for dry agriculture throughout the Mediterranean and much of West-Asia. In summer, when the pressure difference in the North Atlantic Oscillation (NAO) is high, the storms pass further north, leaving the Mediterranean with stable, fair weather, facilitating relatively predictable and safe navigation from May to October (López-Moreno et al., 2011; Pinto et al., 2009; Syed et al., 2010; Ulbrich et al., 2013). Further south, easterly winds, the so-called trade winds, prevail through much of the year, creating the belt of arid regions and deserts dominating Arabia and North Africa (Held, 1989, pp. 46–49).

In the Indian Ocean and the South China Sea, the dominant weather system is known as the monsoons. They blow from the ocean, along East Africa, toward Arabia, South- and East Asia during the northern hemisphere summer. In the northern hemisphere winter, the flow reverses and winds blow from the Asian mainland westwards toward Africa and the sea. Depending on location, this will provide one or two annual periods of rain, determining the growing seasons for different plants and thus the harvest times of different crops (O'Hare, 1997a, 1997b). The monsoon also makes it possible to sail from west to east in the northern-hemisphere summer and from east to west in the northern winter. While maritime communities in the Indian Ocean have made use of the monsoon system at least since the third millennium BCE, the Long Classical Millennium represents a period of intensified maritime connections in the region, arguably peaking in the period from the first century BCE until the second century CE (Fuller et al., 2011; Ray, 2003; Seland, 2014; Sidebotham, 2012).

A belt of mountains known as the Alpide belt runs along the southern edge of the Eurasian tectonic plate, from the Pyrenees to the Hengduan mountains (Fig. 1.1), influencing regional climate regimes, for instance by barring the monsoon rains from reaching Central and Inner Asia. The mountains also make overland movement along the North-South axis cumbersome in many regions and impossible in others. Overland transport remained expensive and slow in the ancient world, even if this could be alleviated through investment in infrastructure, for instance by means of the extensive Roman and Chinese road networks (Adams, 2007; Christopher, 2025; Laurence, 2005). With regard to waterways, the Mediterranean and Indian Ocean connect the landmasses of Europe, Africa and Asia along the west-east axis, while the Red Sea, the Persian Gulf and the Mediterranean provide shorter, but nevertheless useful shortcuts north-south, through the arid and rugged zones of North Africa and West Asia. Large rivers also serve to interconnect the landmasses, in addition to enabling irrigation in arid areas (Abu-Lughod, 1989, pp. 4–49). Their importance to urban networks might be seen by how cities cluster along them. Finally the large steppes and deserts of Eurasia served to interconnect the agricultural regions that supplied the main economic basis of city-life, providing animals for food, transport and war.

Modern maps of ancient trade routes are often deceptive in the manner that they depict communication networks as permanent and clearly marked out infrastructure. They lend the false impression that movement in the ancient world was as easy as getting on the London underground or the North American highway network. These visualizations miss the point that we are often not dealing with roads at all, and never with a steady stream of movement, but with small groups of people and animals that made their way from place to place to place to place at an incredibly slow pace (Seland, 2015). These movements turned into routes by repetition or by routinization as Søren Sindbæk has aptly called it (2008).

Some individuals did cover the distance from China to the Mediterranean and the other way round. One plausible documented instance is the visit of a group of Roman subjects at the Han-court in 166 CE mentioned in Chinese annals (*Hou Hanshu*, 88.12). The visitors arrived to South China by sea, and brought gifts of pearls, rhinoceros horn, aromatic woods and tortoise shells, popular commodities in Indian Ocean trade. Quite many covered several circuits of the network. Abgar of Palmyra is one example, the famous Maes Titianus, who traveled from his native Syria to a place he called the Stone Tower in present-day Uzbekistan, Tajikistan or Xinjiang (Ptolemy, *Geo.* 1.11.7) is another. An enigmatic inscription, reportedly from Kandahar and in Greek language, but composed by an individual with Indian name (Sôphytos)/and patronym (Naratos) speaks relates the life story of a person who earned his fortune through trade in foreign lands, presumably leaving South Asia (Mairs, 2014, pp. 127–135; Pinault, 2005). But most travelers stayed within one part of the system, for instance the Mediterranean or the western Indian Ocean. Maps of ancient trade routes tend to disregard the stops, changes of transport, disconnections and friction that characterized ancient connectivity.

In her *Before European Hegemony*, Janet Abu-Lughod recognized this in conceiving long-distance trade between Asia, Africa and Europe not primarily as lines, but rather as circuits. In her model of the world trade on the eve of the second plague pandemic, in the era of Ibn Batutta and Marco Polo, she described eight macroregional networks connecting the Medieval world (Abu-Lughod, 1989). Adding circuits spanning the Sahara and northwestern Europe, her model may also serve as a visualization of long-distance trade in the early first millennium CE, at the height of Han-, Arsacid and Roman power (Fig. 2.2).

Conceived like this there was no straight road leading from the wall of Hadrian to the Great Wall of China, but a series of interconnected networks that would have to be navigated and changed between. Most of these coincide with one of two things: Either an environmental macroregion like the Mediterranean, the Eurasian Steppe, the Indian Ocean or the Syrian Desert, or alternatively a political unit like the Roman Empire or the Han Empire. At the edge of each network, travelers would have to connect to the next one, usually by adapting to different regimes of seasonality and transport. Where these networks overlapped the hubs of ancient world trade were located, in the form of cities such as Egyptian Alexandria, Syrian Palmyra, Mesopotamian Spasinou Charax, Indian Barygaza, Central Asian Bagram, or Chinese Dunhuang.

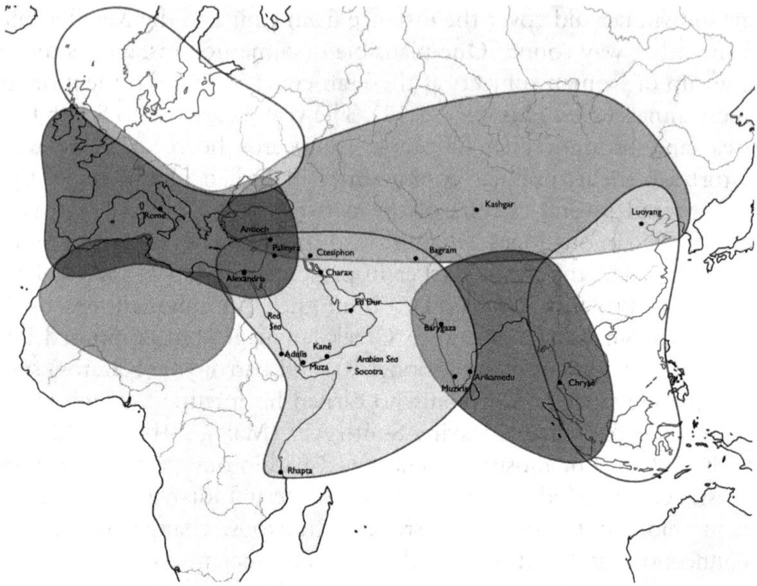

Fig. 2.2 First millennium world trade as macroregional networks and gateway cities. CC BY 4.0 SA

Places and Microregions in Larger Networks: Cyrenaica

To Abu-Lughod, premodern world trade consisted of a series of interconnected networks, each spanning a politically or ecologically determined communication system. Peregrin Horden and Nicholas Purcell, in their paradigm-shaping *The Corrupting Sea*, analyzed one of these macroregional networks, the Mediterranean world, as an agglomeration of microregions. These were small, ecologically heterogeneous areas, for instance incorporating mountains, rivers and plains, integrated by myriads of short-distance, everyday connections on local scale, recurrent, but less frequent interaction with neighboring microregions, and more erratic connections and disconnections with long-distance networks (Horden & Purcell, 2000). One of the case studies they approach in some detail is the Cyrenaica region of present-day Libya, conveniently bordered on three sides by the Mediterranean Sea and to the south by the Sahara Desert, and thus easy to study as a system in its own right (Horden & Purcell, 2000, pp. 65–74).

Cyrenaica is ecologically diverse, ranging from a typical Mediterranean coastal plain offering opportunities for seafaring, fishing and cultivation, to *garrigue*-covered hillsides leading to a well-watered plateau, with extensive tracts of fertile, Mediterranean *terra rossa*, to maqis, hill, and steppe landscapes suitable for sheep and goat pastoralism gradually giving way to sub-desert on the margins (Johnson, 1973, pp. 1–28; Laronde, 1987, pp. 257–314, 1996). In antiquity, it was also known for an enigmatic plant known as *silphium*, much in demand for its medicinal, aphrodisiacal, cosmetic and magical purposes. It was so important and profitable that it was depicted on the coins of the main city of Cyrene, but disappeared, likely due to over-exploitation, in the early period of Roman occupation (Abdelhamed, 2018, pp. 38–46; Gemmill, 1966).

As recounted by Herodotus and collaborated in other Greek sources (Herodotus, *Histories*, book IV; Schaus, 2020), Greek settlers arrived in Cyrenaica in the seventh century BCE, expelling and subjugating the native Libyan population. The Greeks came to know Cyrenaica as the Pentapolis, that is the [Land of] the five cities, after the urban communities of Cyrene, Barca, Taucheira, Ptolemais (pre-Ptolemaic name unknown) and Hesperides (later Berenice, now Benghazi). Each city had their territories with secondary centers, e.g., Apollonia, the port of Cyrene. Early Greek Cyrenaica (Fig. 2.3) may be conceived of as an urban network originally consisting of peer polities, which over time came to center on the two major inland hubs of Barca and Cyrene and eventually on Cyrene alone after extensive inter-city warfare (Johnson, 1973, pp. 94–105: Hdt. Hist. 4.145–158). After 514 BCE Cyrenaica came under outside rule, first as an Achaemenid and later Ptolemaic territory. After an interlude as an independent kingdom ruled by a branch of the Ptolemaic dynasty it became a Roman province, with Cyrene and eventually Apollonia as the main interfaces of imperial networks. Cyrenaican cities, however, continued to function as centers for the collection of agricultural surpluses as well as natural resources such as the coveted silphium (Abdelhamed, 2018). The microregional network of Cyrenaica, held together by a web of roads, tracks and paths converging on Cyrene (Johnson, 1973, pp. 113–120), connected with the macroregional network of the Mediterranean by means of a limited number of gateway nodes situated along the perimeter, that is on the Mediterranean coast. Most importantly Ptolemais and Apollonia, serving as the port cities of Barca and

Cyrene respectively. On a superficial level the network was hierarchical, with economic, demographic and political hierarchies overlapping and probably reinforcing each other.

These networks, based on ecology and topography, shaped and coincided with social networks. We may turn to the example of Synesius of Cyrene, a local notable of the city at the turn of the fifth century CE, who started out as a pagan philosopher, a landowner and member of the local city-council, and ended up first as a an accidental general during a Vandal invasion and later as the bishop of neighboring Ptolemais during the near total breakdown of the imperial network structure of the Roman World in this period (Roques, 1987). We know much about his network from his correspondence, preserved in 159 letters to family, friends, business associates and figures of power in the years 394–413 (Garzya, 2003). Unsurprisingly they reflect the pattern just outlined, showing how he writes to contacts in the gateway cities on the coast in order to receive

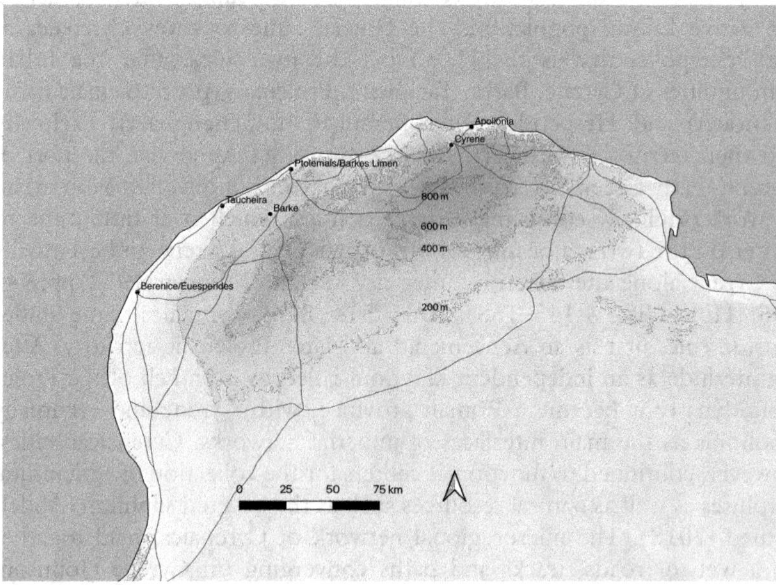

Fig. 2.3 Ancient Cyrenaica with the Archaic Greek city foundations and the Roman period road network. Roads from Ancient World Mapping Centre CC BY 4.0 SA

news and trade products, but also how he himself has access to agricultural and other resources due to his situation at the main hub of the network.

Zooming out to the macroregional level we find ourselves in the Mediterranean Sea. We would expect a microregion like Cyrenaica to be most closely connected to adjacent microregions such as the Nile Delta, as well as Tripolitana in western Libya. Horden and Purcell considered long-distance connections to be secondary to these peer-to-peer contacts between neighboring areas (Horden & Purcell, 2000, pp. 123–172). This certainly seems to be the case in terms of frequency, and volume, but that does not mean that they always were so in terms of importance to the people who engaged in various networks. Irad Malkin, focusing on the Greek Mediterranean in the archaic period, when the network of Greek City states still to a large degree consisted of entities of the same rank, has described the Greek Mediterranean as a small-world-network. Every node was connected to its neighbors, but some maintained contacts directly with more distant nodes and interconnected the entire network to the extent that every node could reach every other node in just a few steps (Malkin, 2011). While most of Synesius' life played out on local and regional scale he was also in contact with people in and traveled to Alexandria, Athens and Constantinople as part of his education and on diplomatic business.

ORBIS, developed by a team at Stanford University, is a geospatial model of the communication network of the Roman World (Meeks, 2015). The Roman world as it appears in ORBIS is not in itself a small-world network, it is probably better described as a hierarchical set of star networks, with its formal layers of political centers from village to city, to provincial capital, and to Rome, or at the time of Synesius other capitals (Constantinople, Ravenna, Milan), with economic resources flowing to the capital as taxes and rent, but also and back toward the provinces mainly as payments to soldiers (Bekker-Nielsen, 1989; Hopkins, 1980). The imperial network, however, was superimposed on and depended on networks based on geography, potentially providing insights into the interaction between different kinds of networks (Fig. 2.4).

Starting with the road network of the Roman Empire, reconstructed on basis of a late Roman map known as *Tabula Peutingeriana* and a small number of route-descriptions known as itineraries, also from Late Antiquity, the old saying that all roads lead to Rome has a certain validity. Roads ran along the borders and from the borders to the provincial capital, from there they connect toward Italy and finally to Rome. In Rome

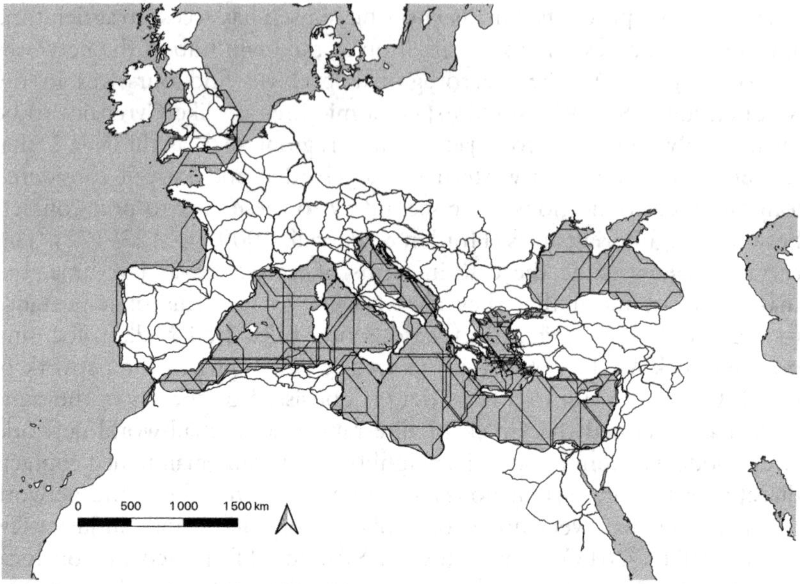

Fig. 2.4 Roman road and maritime networks. Data by Orbis-project/Walter Scheidel, Elijah Meeks, Karl Grossner. CC BY 3.0 SA

stood the famous ***Milliarium Aureum***, the golden milestone, from which all distances in the empire were reckoned (Chevallier, 1976; Rathmann, 2018).

Roads, however, required planning and investment, and even if they were surely beneficial for trade and other kinds of civilian travel, their purpose was to move information, military forces, and economic resources between center and periphery. The maritime network of the Roman empire on the other hand is much closer to a small-world network, where, even if Rome looms large as the central node of both the communication network and the political network, connections between regional hubs short-circuit the hierarchy (Arnaud, 2005).

Thus Cyrenaica, through its maritime gateways of Ptolemais and Apollonia, had connections not only directly toward Rome, but also toward Alexandria, Tripolitana, Crete, Greece and Ilyria. It was this network that allowed Synesius to learn news, communicate with friends, and on occasion travel himself throughout a large part of the eastern Mediterranean.

The Small World of the Western Indian Ocean

Moving east and south of the Mediterranean we find a different network, or circuit, which was never to the same extent supported by a unifying political authority, but which nevertheless played an important role in interconnecting the ancient world, namely the Indian Ocean. Exchange in the Indian Ocean goes back to the third millennium BCE, when documentary sources as well as archaeological finds attest contacts between Mesopotamia and the Indian Subcontinent (Fuller et al., 2011). During the Egyptian Middle Kingdom there is literary, archaeological and iconographic evidence of North-South Contacts in the Red Sea (Kitchen, 2004; Phillips, 1997), as well as genetic evidence for interchange of crops and animals between East Africa and India (Kennedy & Possehl, 2012). Later in the first millennium there is also evidence of crops such as banana and yams moving directly from Southeast Asia to East Africa (Boivin & Fuller, 2009). The basis for this was the same monsoon system that brought the Palmyrene Abgar together with Indian, Greek-speaking and Arab seamen in the Hoq-cave on Socotra.

After the Bronze Age trade and the very early genetic indications of contact. There is traditional archaeological evidence of long-distance exchange only from the third to second centuries BCE onwards (Ray, 2003; Seland, 2014, 2017). The most researched proxy thus far is fine ceramics from South India and Sri Lanka, so-called rouletted ware. These ceramics made their way up both coasts of the Indian Subcontinent, toward the Indus, Narmada, Krishna and Ganges deltas, large river systems that facilitated coast-hinterland integration (Ford et al., 2005; Magee, 2010; Schenk, 2006). This contact is likely also related to the spread of Buddhism in the other direction, from its heartland in the Ganges plain toward the south and particularly to Sri Lanka, as reflected in the Sri Lankan epics and the Jataka stories (Ray, 1998, 2008).

The Greeks, with their penchant for describing the world and recording things in time, were introduced to the Indian Ocean world with the conquests of Alexander the Great. When reports of the Indian Ocean, or more correctly the Arabian Sea, start to reflect in the Mediterranean literary record by the third and second centuries BCE, it is clear that

Indian merchants were already active in the Gulf of Aden, that is present-day Yemen and Somaliland (Ray, 2003; Seland, 2019). Greek-speaking merchants from Egypt gradually linked up with this network, and by the latest in the first century BCE, perhaps before, they were active at least as far south as in Yemen, by the first century CE they also travel to ports situated in Somaliland, and along the entire west coast of India (Casson, 1989), parts of which had long been integrated in Greek urban, intellectual and social networks due to the so-called Indo-Greek kings that expanded southward from the Kabul Valley in the second century BCE (Stoneman, 2019).

The first century CE Greek text known as the *Periplus* (circumnavigation) *of the Erythraean Sea* describes trade and navigation in the Indian Ocean, naming 56 settlements from Egypt to the Bay of Bengal, with emphasis on the Red Sea, the Gulf of Aden and the Arabian Sea (Casson, 1989). The main interest is the possibilities for trade with Egypt, but descriptions of coast and ports also get contain passages that report the presence of ships, sailors and products from Indian, Arabian and African ports, providing a glimpse of different sets of connections that were active in the Indian Ocean at that time.

As recognized by Lionel Casson, the *Periplus* contains two separate route descriptions, related to the itineraries preserved in the Tabula Peutingeriana and in a number of Greek and Roman geographical texts. One goes from Egypt, down the African coast of the Red Sea, along the coasts of Somaliland, Somalia and Kenya, to present-day Tanzania. The second route follows the Arabian west coast from a port called Leukê Komê, "White Village," likely identified with the site of Aynunah, situated in Saudi Arabia close to the border of Jordan (Gawlikowski et al., 2021). The text, mentions, just barely the Persian Gulf, and follows the Indian Coast after that, but becomes increasingly sketchy after rounding the south tip of India (Casson, 1989, pp. 283–291). Conceived as a network every settlement is connected only with those adjacent to it. The result would be a linear network not unlike a modern railway or subway map. However, like in the Mediterranean, ships also crossed the open sea. If we add the direct connections between ports described in the Periplus, between African, Arabian, South Asian and Southeast Asian ports, we end up with a quite different impression, which has elements of a small-world network: While most ports were only connected to their neighbors, but some hubs were better connected, making sure that the whole network could be reached within a few steps (Seland, 2016b) (Fig. 2.5).

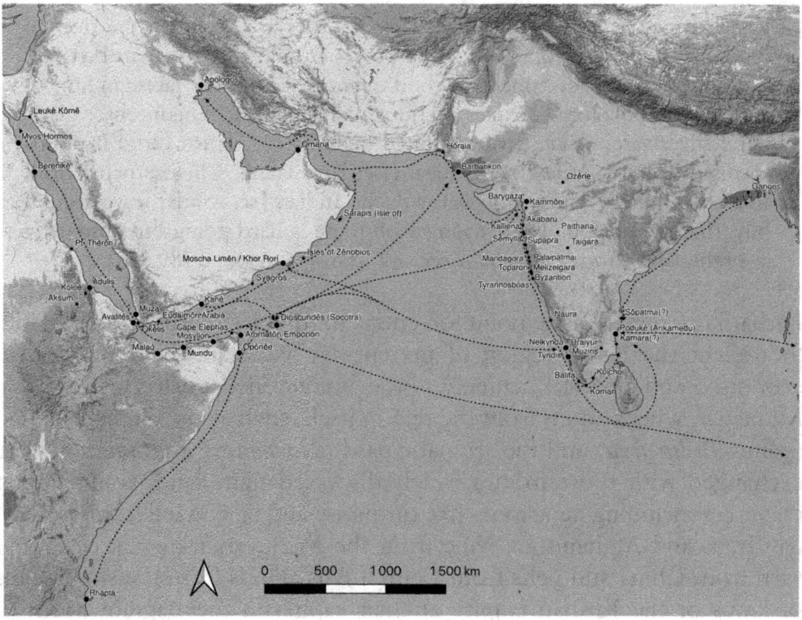

Fig. 2.5 Nodes, hubs and connections between them mentioned in the Periplus Maris Erythraei. Basemap CAWM. CC BY 4.0

Dynamic Hinterlands

As with the Cyrenaica microregion of the Mediterranean, the western Indian Ocean also provides opportunities to investigate hinterland dynamics. Each of the settlements along the Indian Ocean coastlines served as gateways into hinterland networks. Most of these coastal settlements were small and maintained purposefully in order to serve as a place of exchange. They facilitated communication with political and agricultural centers in the hinterland, and in the same manner as in Cyrenaica, there is a clear hierarchy between these centers, one of them ranking higher in the hierarchy than the others (Seland, 2007).

A case in point is the port of Barbarikon, at the mouth of the Indus, perhaps identifiable with the fortified coastal site of Banbhore in present-day Pakistan (Manassero & Fiorani, 2014). Here the anonymous author of the *Periplus* gives the following description of conditions prevailing in the second half of the first century CE:

> Vessels moor at Barbarikon, but all the cargoes are taken up the river to the king at the metropolis. In this port of trade there is a market for: clothing, with no adornment in good quantity, of printed fabric in limited quantity; multicolored textiles; peridot; coral; storax; frankincense; glassware; silverware; money; wine, limited quantity. As return cargo it offers: costus; bdellium; *lykion*; nard; turquoise; lapis lazuli; Chinese pelts, cloth and yarn; indigo. Those who sail with the Indian [sc. winds] leave around July, that is Epheiph. The crossing with these is hard going but absolutely favorable and shorter. (*Periplus* sec. 39, transl. Casson, 1989, 75)

Barbarikon served as a point of entry to the Indo-Parthian kingdom located in the Sindh region of present-day Pakistan. The commercial, economic and political center was the unidentified upstream capital of Minnagar, where goods from the region itself, such as the pigment indigo (genus *Indigofera*) and the aromatic nard (*Nardostachys jatamansi*) were exchanged with those from a widely dispersed hinterland, commanding resources including gemstones like turquoise and lapis lazuli from present-day Iran, and Afghanistan, wine from the Mediterranean, silk cloth and yarn from China and pelts from Central Asia. Finds from the storerooms of kings of the Kushan empire at their capital in the Bagram north of Kabul, discovered undisturbed by French archaeologists in 1938, show a further node in the network, c. 1500 km upriver and inland, and across the Khyber Pass connecting South and Central Asia. Here Bronzes and Roman glass from Egypt were stored along with exquisitely carved Indian ivories (Cambon, 2011; Mehendale, 2011). Whether hoarded by the Kushan ruler or awaiting further exchange, they attest to the scale, wealth and political significance of ancient long-distance networks.

As the presence of Chinese silk at the mouth of the Indus River shows, these networks spanned the entirety of the immense Eurasian landmass. From Bagram tracks lead across the Hindu Kush to the Oxus river, that separated the historical landscapes of Bactria from those of Sogdiana and further north Ferghana. By following the tributaries of the Oxus or the Jaxartes eastwards into the Pamir range and along mountain paths that in places ran more than 3000 m above sea level, it was possible to reach the oasis of Kashgar at the western edge of the Tarim Basin in modern Xinjiang. As the name implies, the Tarim Basin is a topographical depression without any outlet. It is of immense size, spanning c. 1500 km east-west and 400–600 km north-south. Due to the long distance to the sea and the tall mountains surrounding it, it receives almost no rain, but while the center of the region is dominated by the hyper-arid Taklamakan Desert, rivers and subterranean aquifers descending from the mountains allowed permanent habitation and irrigated agriculture along the edges and rivers. Here a chain of small kingdoms ruled by princes of Buddhist leanings, utilizing Kharosthi script, emerged in the period around the turn of the common era, some of them several hundred kilometers of inhospitable desert from their nearest neighbors (Høisæter, 2023b). Paying at least symbolic respect to Kushan, later Sasanid and Chinese imperial overlords, these mostly autonomous city states provided possibilities for communication eastwards to Dunhuang, the westernmost outpost under direct Chinese imperial control (Høisæter, 2023a).

The arid dunes of the Taklamakan are in some respects not entirely dissimilar from the Indian Ocean and the Mediterranean Sea. For some they constituted inhospitable areas that needed to be traversed. At sea travelers had to figure out the safe and fast passages, on land they needed to know the situation of mountain passes and find the waterholes. As in the Mediterranean and the Indian Ocean linear network patterns evolved along the edges of the Tarim Basin, serving east-west communication, but there were also opportunities for short-circuiting the network, opening the opportunities for more complex peer polity interaction and turning these strings of small city states into small-world networks in their own right.

Communication, Environment, Seasonality

As argued above, not only settlement, but also communication in the premodern world was to a large extent determined by the environment. While this insight is hardly novel, it is rarely taken into account in scholarship on premodern trade. Seasonal patterns influencing communication and movement were not limited to the monsoon system in the Indian Ocean. Shipping came to a near standstill in the Mediterranean winter, in order to avoid the frequent and hazardous winter storms. This does not imply that it was impossible to sail in the winter, but that few would do so without good reasons (Arnaud, 2005; Beresford, 2013). The seasonal weather patterns were not identical with, but nevertheless quite compatible with the agricultural production cycle of important commercial crops, which would be complete in late fall (wine), early winter (olive oil) and spring (grain) and thus ready for export when the next sailing season commenced. Textile production was also traditionally undertaken in winter, when agricultural work came to a near stop. Overland travel similarly became cumbersome in the winter months, as rain turned hard soil into mud, also in semi-arid regions like most of West Asia. In Central Asia snow would make mountain passages impossible and in the Tarim Basin temperatures would be freezing. The network nature of ancient exchange and the shaping agency of the natural environment came together to define and structure micro- and macroregional networks of places of production, transit and exchange. This implies that ancient long-distance exchange consisted of series of networks that were certainly influenced by politics and technology, but for which different environmental regimes formed the basis. Approaching communication as networks rather than simply as movement makes it more evident how such systems interacted, and how they operated on different scales, from domestic through local, regional and supra-regional to proto-global.

Ancient networks of communication and exchange were also urban networks. Cities and other central places provided the nodes that connected networks on different scale. Cities provided points of transit and transition; places to rest, trade and change mode of transport. Cities were places to buy products for consumption or export and to sell products imported from economic hinterlands, distant as well as nearby. Returning to the map of old-world trade at the turn of the third century CE, inspired by Abu-Lughods map of the world system a millennium later (Fig. 2.2), each of these economic circuits represent interconnected small-world networks in themselves, and each of the connect to other circuits by means of cities.

References

Abdelhamed, M. H. (2018). *The economic condition of the main Cyrenaican cities (North-Eastern Libya) from the Hellenistic to the mid-Roman period: Textual analysis* (PhD. University of Leicester).

Abu-Lughod, J. L. (1989). *Before European hegemony: The world system A.D. 1250–1350*. Oxford University Press.

Adams, C. (2007). *Land transport in Roman Egypt: A study of economics and administration in a Roman province*. Oxford University Press.

Arnaud, P. (2005). *Les routes de la navigation antique: Itinéraires en Méditerranée*. Éditions Errance.

Bekker-Nielsen, T. (1989). *The geography of power: Studies in the urbanization of Roman North-West Europe*. B.A.R.

Beresford, J. (2013). *The ancient sailing season*. Brill.

Boivin, N., & Fuller, D. Q. (2009). Shell middens, ships and seeds: Exploring coastal subsistence, maritime trade and the dispersal of domesticates in and around the ancient Arabian Peninsula. *Journal of World Prehistory, 22*(2), 113–180.

Braudel, F. (1981). *Civilization and capitalism, 15th–18th century: The structure of everyday life*. University of California Press.

Cambon, P. (2011). Begram: Alexandria of the Caucasus, capital of the Kushan Empire. In F. Hiebert & P. Cambon (Eds.), *Afghanistan: Crossroads of the ancient world* (pp. 145–161). British Museum.

Casson, L. (1989). *The Periplus Maris Erythraei*. Princeton University Press.

Casson, L. (1994). *Travel in the ancient world*. Johns Hopkins University Press.

Chevallier, R. (1976). *Roman roads*. B.T. Batsford.

Christopher, J. (2025). Roads to empire: On roadbuilding traditions in ancient Rome and early China. *Journal of Ancient History, 13*(1), 119–158.

Ford, L. A., Pollard, A. M., Coningham, R. A. E., & Stern, B. (2005). A geochemical investigation of the origin of Rouletted and other related South Asian fine wares. *Antiquity, 79*(306), 909–920.

Fuller, D. Q., Boivin, N., Hoogervorst, T., & Allaby, R. (2011). Across the Indian Ocean: The prehistoric movement of plants and animals. *Antiquity, 85*, 544–558.

Garzya, A. (2003). *Synésios de Cyrène*. Les Belles Lettres.

Gawlikowski, M., Juchniewicz, K., & al-Zahrani, A. (Eds.). (2021). *Aynuna. A Nabataean port on the Red Sea. Seven seasons of Saudi-Polish excavations (2014–2018)*. Polish Centre of Mediterranean Archaeology, University of Warsaw.

Gemmill, C. L. (1966). Silphium. *Bulletin of the History of Medicine, 40*(4), 295–313.

Gorea, M. (2012). Palmyra and Socotra. In I. Strauch (Ed.), *Foreign sailors on Socotra: The inscriptions and drawings from the Cave Hoq* (pp. 447–487). Hempen.

Hartmann, U. (2024). Palmyra and the third-century crisis. In R. Raja (Ed.), *The Oxford handbook of Palmyra* (pp. 143–160). Oxford University Press.

Held, C. C. (1989). *Middle East patterns: Places, peoples, and politics*. Westview Press.

Hildebrandt, B. (2017). Silk production and trade in the Roman Empire. In B. Hildebrandt & C. Gillis (Eds.), *Silk: Trade & exchange along the Silk Roads between Rome and China in antiquity* (pp. 71–93). Oxbow Books.

Hopkins, K. (1980). Taxes and trade in the Roman Empire 200 BC–AD 400. *Journal of Roman Studies, 70*, 101–125.

Horden, P., & Purcell, N. (2000). *The corrupting sea: A study of Mediterranean history*. Blackwell.

Høisæter, T. L. (2023a). Islands in a sea of sand: The role of Tarim Basin polities in global trade during late antiquity. *Journal of Global History, 18*(3), 401–425.

Høisæter, T. L. (2023b). Trade, Buddhism, and the Kushan connection: Exchange across the Pamir Knot and the making of the Silk Roads, 2nd century BCE to 5th century CE. In *Oxford research encyclopedia of Asian history*. https://doi.org/10.1093/acrefore/9780190277727.013.598

Johnson, D. L. (1973). *Jabal al-Akhdar, Cyrenaica: An historical geography of settlement and livelihood*. University of Chicago Department of Geography.

Kennedy, K. A. R., & Possehl, G. L. (2012). Were there commercial communications between prehistoric Harappans and African populations? *Advances in Anthropology, 2*(4), 169–180.

Kitchen, K. A. (2004). The elusive land of Punt revisited. In P. Lunde, A. Porter, & S. J. Simpson (Eds.), *Trade and travel in the Red Sea region. Proceedings of the Red Sea Project I* (pp. 25–31). Archaeopress.

Laronde, A. (1987). *Cyrène et la Libye hellénistique – Libykai Historiai – de l'époque républicaine au principat d'Auguste*.

Laronde, A. (1996). L'exploitation de la chôra cyrénéenne à l'époque classique et hellénistique. *Comptes Rendus des Séances De L'académie des Inscriptions Et Belles-Lettres, 140*(2), 503–527.

Laurence, R. (2005). Land transport in Roman Italy: Costs, practice and the economy. In H. Parkins & C. Smith (Eds.), *Trade, traders and the ancient city* (pp. 143–162). Routledge.

López-Moreno, J. I., Vicente-Serrano, S. M., Morán-Tejeda, E., Lorenzo-Lacruz, J., Kenawy, A., & Beniston, M. (2011). Effects of the North Atlantic Oscillation (NAO) on combined temperature and precipitation winter modes in the Mediterranean mountains: Observed relationships and projections for the 21st century. *Global and Planetary Change, 77*(1), 62–76.

Magee, P. (2010). Revisiting Indian Rouletted ware and the impact of Indian Ocean trade in early historic South Asia. *Antiquity, 84*(326), 1043–1054.

Mairs, R. (2014). *The Hellenistic far east: Archaeology, language, and identity in Greek Central Asia*.

Malkin, I. (2011). *A small Greek world: Networks in the ancient Mediterranean*. Oxford University Press.

Manassero, N., & Fiorani, V. P. (2014). The site of Banbhore (Sindh–Pakistan): A joint Pakistani-French-Italian project. Current research in archaeology and history (2010–2014). *The Silk Road, 12*, 82–88.

Meeks, E. (2015). The design and implementation of ORBIS: The Stanford geospatial network model of the Roman world. *Bulletin of the Association for Information Science and Technology, 41*(2), 17–21.

Mehendale, S. (2011). Begram catalogue. In F. Hiebert & P. Cambon (Eds.), *Afghanistan: Crossroads of the ancient world* (pp. 162–209). British Museum Press.

O'Hare, G. (1997a). The Indian monsoon Part 1: The wind system. *Geography, 82*(3), 218–230.

O'Hare, G. (1997b). The Indian monsoon Part 2: The rains. *Geography, 82*(4), 335–352.

Phillips, J. (1997). Punt and Aksum: Egypt and the Horn of Africa. *Journal of African Studies, 38*(3), 423–457.

Pinault, G.-J. (2005). Remarques sur les noms propres d'origine indienne dans la stèle de Sôphytos. In O. Bopearachchi & M.-F. Boussac (Eds.), *Afghanistan: Ancien carrefour entre l'est et l'ouest* (Vol. 3, pp. 137–142). Brepols.

Pinto, J. G., Zacharias, S., Fink, A. H., Leckebusch, G. C., & Ulbrich, U. (2009). Factors contributing to the development of extreme North Atlantic cyclones and their relationship with the NAO. *Climate Dynamics, 32*(5), 711–737.

Rathmann, M. (2018). *Tabula Peutingeriana: Die einzige Weltkarte aus der Antike*. WBG, Philipp von Zabern.

Ray, H. P. (1998). *The winds of change—Buddhism and the maritime links of early South Asia*. Oxford University Press.

Ray, H. P. (2003). *The archaeology of seafaring in ancient South Asia*. Cambridge University Press.

Ray, H. P. (2008). The axial age in Asia: The archaeology of Buddhism (500 B.C.–A.D. 500). In M. T. Stark (Ed.), *Archaeology of Asia* (pp. 303–323). Blackwell.

Roques, D. (1987). *Synésios de Cyrène et la Cyrénaïque du Bas-Empire*. Editions du Centre national de la recherche scientifique: Presses du CNRS, diffusion.

Schaus, G. P. (2020). Cyrenaica. In F. Angelis (Ed.), *A companion to Greeks across the ancient world* (pp. 339–362). Wiley.

Schenk, H. (2006). The dating and historical value of Rouletted Ware. *Zeitschrift Für Archäologie Aussereuropäischer Kulturen, 1*, 123–152.

Seland, E. H. (2007). Red Sea and Indian Ocean: Ports and their hinterland. In J. Starkey, P. Starkey, & T. J. Wilkinson (Eds.), *Natural resources and cultural connections of the Red Sea* (pp. 211–218). Archaeopress.

Seland, E. H. (2011). The Persian Gulf or the Red Sea? Two axes in ancient Indian Ocean trade, where to go and why. *World Archaeology, 43*(3), 398–409.

Seland, E. H. (2014). Archaeology of trade in the western Indian Ocean, 300 BC–AD 700. *Journal of Archaeological Research, 22*(4), 367–406.

Seland, E. H. (2015). Writ in water, lines in sand: Ancient trade routes, models and comparative evidence. *Cogent Humanities, 2*, 1110272.

Seland, E. H. (2016a). *Ships of the desert and ships of the sea: Palmyra in the world trade of the first three centuries CE*. Harrassowitz.

Seland, E. H. (2016b). The Periplus of the Erythraean Sea: A network approach. *Asian Review of World History, 4*(2), 191–206.

Seland, E. H. (2017). The archaeological record of Indian Ocean engagements in the Red Sea. In *Oxford Handbooks Online*. Oxford University Press. https://doi.org/10.1093/oxfordhb/9780199935413.001.0001/oxfordhb-9780199935413-e-51

Seland, E. H. (2019). Als Indien das Römische Reich entdeckte: Exploration und Handel im Indischen Ozean vom Osten aus gesehen. In R. Schultz (Ed.), *Maritime Entdeckung und Expansion. Kontinuitäten, Parallelen und Brüche von der Antike bis in die Neuzeit* (Vol. 77, pp. 109–120). De Gruyter Oldenbourg.

Sidebotham, S. E. (2012). The Red Sea and the Indian Ocean in the age of the great empires. In D. T. Potts (Ed.), *A companion to the archaeology of the ancient Near East* (pp. 1041–1059). Blackwell.

Sindbæk, S. (2008). Routes and long-distance traffic: The nodal points of Wulfstan's voyage. In A. Englert & A. Trakadas (Eds.), *Wulfstan's voyage: Maritime culture of the North* (pp. 72–78). The Viking Ship Museum.

Stoneman, R. (2019). *The Greek experience of India: From Alexander to the Indo-Greeks*. Princeton University Press.

Strauch, I. (2012). *Foreign sailors on Socotra: The inscriptions and drawings from the Cave Hoq*. Hempen.

Syed, F. S., Giorgi, F., Pal, J. S., & Keay, K. (2010). Regional climate model simulation of winter climate over Central-Southwest Asia, with emphasis on NAO and ENSO effects. *International Journal of Climatology: A Journal of the Royal Meteorological Society, 30*(2), 220–235.

Ulbrich, U., Xoplaki, E., Dobricic, S., García-Herrera, R., Lionello, P., Adani, M., Baldi, M., Barriopedro, D., Coccimiglio, P., & Dalu, G. (2013). Past and current climate changes in the Mediterranean region. In A. Navarra & L. Tubiana (Eds.), *Regional assessment of climate change in the Mediterranean* (pp. 9–51). Springer.

Van Rensburg, J. J. (2016). *The maritime traditions of the fishermen of Socotra*. Archaeopress.

Wild, J. P., Wild, F. C., & Clapham, A. J. (2008). Roman cotton revisited. In C. Alfaro Giner & L. Karali (Eds.), *Textiles and dyes in antiquity. Vestidos, textiles y tintes: Estudios sobre la producción de bienes de consumo en la antigüedad: Actas del II Symposium Internacional sobre Textiles y Tintes del Mediterráneo en el Mundo Antiguo (Atenas, 24 al 26 de noviembre, 2005)* (pp. 143–147). Universitat de València.

CHAPTER 3

People

Abstract This chapter shifts the attention to social networks and starts with discussing the problem of creating and maintaining trust, which was a major obstacle to long-distance trade and cross-cultural interaction in the ancient world. It introduces key terminology from New Institutional Economics before moving on to discussing trade diasporas as forms of social networks. Janet Landa's work on Ethnically Homogenous Middlemen Groups and clublike organizations as solutions to the problem of trust is outlined, and its applicability on ancient evidence is argued on cases drawn from the forensic orations of Demosthenes (fourth century BCE) as well as on evidence of religious and professional associations in the ancient Mediterranean, West Asia and South Asia.

Keywords Trust · Social Networks · New Institutional Economics · Trade diasporas · Kinship · Religion · Ethnicity

At the outset of his history of the *Peloponnesian War,* maybe the most famous work of history ever written, Thucydides, describes what he took to be the relatively recent past:

© The Author(s), under exclusive license to Springer Nature Switzerland AG 2026

E. H. Seland, *Long-Distance Trade in the Ancient World*, Palgrave Studies in Ancient Economies,
https://doi.org/10.1007/978-3-031-90855-2_3

> There was no trade, no secure communications with each other by land or sea. Each group grazed its own land for subsistence, not building up financial reserves or farming the land, as it was never known when someone else might attack and take it from them–besides, there were no walls. Thucydides, *History of the Peloponnesian war* 1.2.2, transl. Hammond (2021)

Thucydides saw the past as a world in which local, close-knit networks dominated. These were based on strong ties, including presumably, even if this is not stated explicitly in the cited passage, of perceived common ancestry, shared institutions and communal action. While trust would prevail within the group, it would be lacking toward outsiders. In Thucydides' imagined past there was no trade, no travel and no stability, as other groups might attack at any time.

Thucydides lived at the outset of what we call the Long Classical Millennium in this book. The historical past that he claimed to describe corresponds to what modern scholars have somewhat dismissively referred to as Dark Age Greece, due to the fact that the period has left us no contemporary, written evidence. While it is unlikely that Thucydides had detailed and correct knowledge about this period, the rhetorical message he is conveying is that this past, whether real or imagined, was fundamentally different from his own time. Thucydides is describing the so-called "Natural State," to borrow a term famously used by Thomas Hobbes in his *Leviathan* (1651), by which he meant human existence before the establishment of a social order. This was a time, when in the words of Hobbes, there were "[n]o arts; no letters; no society; and which is worst of all, continual fear and danger of violent death; and the life of man, solitary, poor, nasty, brutish, and short" (Hobbes, 1651, pt 1 ch. 12). Considering that Hobbes was also the earliest translator of Thucydides into English (1628), he was likely directly inspired by the latter in his description of the Natural State (Klosko & Rice, 1985). Also, there is good reason to assume that such a thing as the Natural State described by Hobbes never actually existed. Our ability to work together in groups, to form social networks, seems to be a trait that characterizes us as a species. In Yuval Harari's global history blockbuster *Sapiens*, the ability to expand these networks is seen as facilitated by the creation of "imagined orders," a term very similar to that of "imagined communities," coined by historian of nationalism Benedict Anderson (Anderson, 1991; Harari, 2015). Recent work demonstrates that such networks took on a huge variety of forms in different parts of the world and at different times and that there is little reason to draw strict lines between complex societies and others (Graeber & Wengrow, 2021). However, we do not have to accept Thucydides' and Hobbes' bleak image of pre- or non-state society to appreciate the problems that emerge when social orders collapse. Current world affairs continuously illustrate the atrocities that people are able and even eager to inflict on others that they do not perceive to belong to their own group, even if they do maintain a strict social order within their own groups.

Throughout history the task of establishing social order has been filled by political organizations, be they tribes, states, merchant companies or criminal groups. This terminology deliberately draws on the academic discipline of New Institutional Economics, which deals with the influence of social institutions on economic relations. Douglass C. North was arguably the scholar who went the furthest in developing New Institutional Economics as a historical theory (North, 1990; North et al., 2009). He analyzed societies as consisting of organizations and institutions. By organizations he described 'groups of people pursuing a mix of individual and common goals through partly coordinated behaviour' (2009, p. 15). In the premodern world such organizations were mostly political in the sense that they specialised in rent-seeking behaviour through the use and containment of violence. There were no private firms and no voluntary associations in the modern sense of these words, although, as we shall see below, alternative forms of social organization intended to foster cohesion did exist in the ancient world (Seland, 2023b). Rent-seeking is the act of extracting resources by manipulating the social environment rather than by creating wealth, for instance through taxation, extortion, land rents or tribute. Typical examples of rent-seeking organizations in early history include states, tribes and robber gangs, who were closed-access or members-only groups, who used, threatened to use or chose to abstain from using violence in order to raise economic resources that were redistributed among their members. Such organizations were also social networks with shared ties among their members. Systems dominated by such groups are called Natural States by North et al. (2009), no doubt with reference to Hobbes.

According to North, interaction, both within and between organizations, takes place by means of institutions. By institutions North described what he called "the rules of the game," the patterns of interaction that govern and constrain the relationships of individuals" (North et al.,

2009, p. 15). Institutions may include informal ties such as friendship and kinship; communal practices, e.g., worship, but also formal codes of law. In network terminology we might say that institutions describe the edges that connect the nodes of the network. The early Greek world as described by Thucydides was a world that lacked institutions that facilitated non-violent interaction between members of different organizations.

As argued in Chapter 2, premodern world trade consisted of overlapping macroregional trading networks, for instance the Mediterranean, the Western Indian Ocean and Central Asia. These were defined primarily by climate and environment and secondarily by integration into political organizations such as the Roman, Arsacid and Han empires, but actual trading operations were facilitated by social networks of producers, traders, consumers and rulers. This chapter discusses how institutions facilitating non-violent interaction within and between such networks were established in long-distance and cross-cultural trade in the ancient world.

Trading Diasporas and Social Networks

Social networks of cross-cultural traders in the premodern world are generally described as trading diasporas. The concept was introduced by Abner Cohen, who studied the organization of trade in contemporary West Africa, and was developed into a universal model of premodern cross-cultural trade by Philip Curtin (Cohen, 1971; Curtin, 1984). A trading diaspora is a group of merchants settled permanently or semi-permanently abroad, in order to engage in trade, while maintaining their identification with and orientation toward a homeland, whether real or imagined (Curtin, 1984; Seland, 2016). Well-attested historical examples include Assyrian traders in Middle Bronze Age Karum Kanesh (Larsen, 2000; Veenhof, 2013), Palmyrenes in southern Mesopotamia (Seland, 2023a), the Medieval German Hanse in Northern Europe, and the many overseas' trading companies of early modern Europe. The term has been challenged by Aslanian, who pointed out that the homeland is only present in a very symbolic sense, if even that, in cases such as the Armenian diaspora of the early modern period studied by him, or also in the Jewish and Greek diasporas of the Mediterranean and Indian Ocean in the ancient period. Aslanian suggested instead the term "circulation societies" (2011), which probably has a wider applicability than Curtin's model, but which does not exclude the existence of diaspora communities. Trading diasporas were also seen by Curtin to be operating across cultures. This might miss institutional solutions to similar challenges of cross-group and long-distance interaction taking place within political and cultural frameworks as for instance the Greek or Roman Mediterranean or the Han Empire, where cultural dividing lines were less aligned with political borders. Treating Trading diasporas, Circulation societies and Organizations in the sense of North et al. as varieties of social networks, allows us to escape this problem of fitting past communities into modern categories, and study how these groups interacted among themselves and with people they considered to be outsiders.

While network analysis as well as New Institutional Economics have become staple tools for the study of ancient economies in recent years (Bang, 2008; Droß-Krüpe et al., 2016; Evers, 2011; Scheidel et al., 2007; von Reden & Kowalzig, 2022), the question of how relations in social networks are established in practice remains understudied. A major theoretical contribution to the study of trust, identity and ethnicity is the work of economist Janet T. Landa (Landa, 1994; Wickström & Landa, 2018). Her point of departure is the study of how trust can be established in cases where no binding contract is possible. While we have detailed information on dealings within groups all the way back to the Old Assyrian period (Dercksen, 2014), no binding contract existed in dealings between groups, at least not a priori. Contract here refers to any binding agreement and does not necessarily involve written documents, although that would often be the case. In absence of ways of enforcing such agreements, trust needed to be established (Reinard & Rollinger, 2023; Seland, 2023b).

Landa has studied how trust is established in more recent history by means of social networks called Ethnically Homogenous Middlemen Groups. The theoretical basis for her model is partly that of New Institutional Economics, with the main question being how the problem of transaction costs may be dealt with. Additional sources of inspiration include the social anthropological work of Clifford Geertz and Richard Posner. Geertz studied bazaar trade in Morocco in the 1960s and 1970s. He noted that uncertainty and lack of information led to commercial relations mutating into social ties. Merchants and customers would deal with each other repeatedly. This process he called 'clientalization' (Geertz, 1978; Landa, 1994, p. 102). Posner, working in West Africa in the same period, noted that uncertainty in economic transactions was mitigated by repeated dealings between buyers and sellers, who over time developed social ties such as friendships and even pseudo-kinships (Posner, 1980). Ancient economies display many of the same traits of uncertainty, imperfect information and weak integration, as demonstrated by Peter Bang, in his *The Roman Bazaar* (2008).

Landa draws on economic theory on clubs and clublike organizations, which she defined as "any voluntary group deriving mutual benefit from the reduction of contract uncertainty" (1994, p. 117). To Landa clubs are somewhat similar to North's organizations, and include families, clans, ethnic and religious groups (1994, pp. 126–135). In this they also encompass Trading diasporas and Circulation societies in the sense of Curtin and Aslanian discussed above. Landa's model was based on the Hokkien Chinese, a community originating in the Fujian province of south-eastern China, but since at least the fifteenth century settled across Southeast Asia, where they have continued to engage in commerce until today (Conceicao, 2016). According to Landa, Hokkien distinguish their business relations between (1) near kin, (2) distant kin, (3) clansmen, (4) people originating from the same village in China, (5) fellow Hokkien Chinese, (6) other Chinese and (7) others. Contract uncertainty and thus transaction costs increase as relations proceed outwards through these circles of in-groups and becomes larger as more agents join the transactional networks (1994, pp. 102–107).

Dealing with family members carries the least risk within this framework, but even that is not risk-free, and the ambitious merchant will want to deal also with more distant members of the social network or even outsiders. For agents aiming to participate in long-distance or cross-cultural trade, this is a precondition. After outlining her model Landa goes on to describe how the establishment of clublike arrangements might alleviate uncertainty and lack of information, and lead to the establishment of trust instead. Among the Hokkien Chinese, trust is produced by institutions such as personal names, clan names, ethnic identities, religious identities, insignia and signs (1994, pp. 124–135). Personal names and group names carry reputations that precede and outlast economic transactions. Reputation is accumulated over time, and the social and economic costs resulting from loss of reputation must be balanced against any short-term economic benefits of breaching contract and may have repercussions on group level. Trust is frequently established by distinguishing between insiders and outsiders (Endreß, 2023). Extended kinship groups, such as clans, use surnames and patronyms for this purpose, and group identity becomes an important intangible asset that might be lost in case of breach of contract. On the other hand, kinship might be extended through institutions such as marriage, blood-brotherhood, fictive relations or even lying (Landa, 1994, pp. 126–130). On a more general level, ethnic identity is not primarily about shared in-group ties, but rather about maintaining borders toward other groups (Barth, 1969; Brubaker, 2002). Ancient societies were often multicultural, but with low degree of assimilation between groups. Ethnicity could be an easy way of identifying shared group membership, as it tends to correlate with appearance, language, diet and dress (Landa, 1994, pp. 130–131). Finally, religious groups also have clublike qualities, for instance in fostering cohesion and solidarity between group members through rituals and shared beliefs, while also imposing membership costs, e.g., through marriage restrictions and dietary rules that make it easier to interact with group members than with outsiders (1994, pp. 131–134). These ways in which trust was established and reinforcing trust through intragroup interaction also have implications for our understanding of how ancient trade operated by means of social networks (Seland, 2023b).

Creating Trust

An illustration of the importance of names and reputations is contained in one of the speeches of the Athenian orator Demosthenes (384–322 BCE), dealing with an early example of identity theft (Oration 39, *Against Boiôtos in regard to his name*). The speech was written on behalf of a certain Mantitheos (1) son of Mantias, who is suing his half-brother Boiôtos, for also calling himself Mantitheos (2). Boiothôs, to his defense, is claiming that he, being the oldest of the two, has the right to carry the name of their common paternal grandfather regardless of their given names.

According to Demosthenes' oration, which only gives the version of the claimant, Mantitheos (1) had been entered into the rolls of the *phratry,* "brotherhood" at infancy, in accordance with Athenian law. The phratry was the basic social unit of the Athenian state, and had the important gatekeeping-task of recognizing citizenship, which was restricted to children of two free Athenians (Jones, 1999, p. 199). His half-brother, whom he accused of identity theft, had only been recognized by his father at some point during his childhood, and had been inscribed in the *phratry* under the name of Boiôtos (Dem. *Or.* 39.21). When, however, Boiôtos at a later stage, and after the death of their common father, was entered into the rolls of the *demê*, the basic political unit, which was based on local community rather than kinship, he did so under the name of Mantitheos (2) (Dem. *Or.* 39.22). When, as the original Mantitheos (1) holds forth, two persons belonging to the same *phylê* and *demê* also carried the same name and patronym, there was no legal way to discern them save litigation. If one of them was drafted for military service, public duty, summoned to court, sentenced to a fine or defaulted on his credit, who was to be responsible (Dem. *Or.* 39.7–19)? The brief example, not without relevance even in the digital age, shows that name as well as kinship were vital intangible assets that could give access to economic, social and political resources. It also shows that in Athens, probably also in many other ancient societies, these were legal entities. Name and kinship could be obtained and confirmed by legal means, opening the opportunity also for this happening without justification, which is what the claimant asserts that has happened in this case.

The use of near kin and household members as agents in long-distance trade is well attested in the ancient world and indeed in any premodern setting. All the way back to the Karum Kanesh archives documenting trade between Anatolia and Northern Mesopotamia in the Middle Bronze Age, cases of near kin doing business together, for instance with a brother, son or nephew acting as agent, are well attested (Dercksen, 2014; Larsen, 2000; Veenhof, 2013). In the Roman period inscriptional evidence of Palmyrene caravans between Syria and Mesopotamia reveals that although leadership of caravans was a civic office, leadership seems to have rotated among elite families, with a disproportionate number of caravan leaders being related to others who had held the office on an earlier occasion (Seland, 2024). This is a solution to what economic theory describes as the principal-agent-problem. In situations with imperfect information, ubiquitous in ancient long-distance trade, economic actors, 'principals,' need to rely on agents with potentially conflicting self-interest. When relying on household members, emotional, legal and social obligations run parallel with economic ties, thus increasing trust and reducing costs connected with monitoring and enforcement. In the Greco-Roman world, we find numerous examples of slaves and freedmen acting as agents, often with the opportunity to carry on economic activity of their own on the side, which allowed them to align their self-interest with that of their master or in this case principal. A well-known example is preserved in a different oration of Demosthenes (34, *Against Phormio*), where the claimant Chrysippus kept a slave in Cimmerian Bosporus in order to look after business interests (Dem. *Or.*34). The maintenance of a slave in a foreign town would entail a substantial cost, but one incurred by Chrysippus in order to avoid breach of trust with other business partners. That this was common throughout the ancient period is supported by late Roman law accounting for the possibility of shipmasters being slaves and thus not legally liable for loss or damage to passengers or property (*Digesta* 14, 1, 1, 4). From the Indian Ocean, the anonymous *Periplus of the Erythraean Sea,* discussed in more detail in preceding chapters, reports that merchants from Mouza in present-day Yemen sent out agents that settled in ports on eh East African coast and married local women, thus establishing a social as well as a physical foothold in local communities (*Periplus* sec. 16). Later period merchants, belonging to Jewish, Armenian and Hadrami trading networks in the Indian Ocean ports also frequently stationed family members in foreign ports in order to carry out business (Aslanian, 2011; Manger, 2010; Margariti, 2007).

Families, in premodern settings better labeled as households, were flexible in the respect that they also included people who were not related by blood. While most ancient societies we are familiar with were concerned with group membership, inheritance and legitimacy, they also maintained a range of social and legal institutions that allowed the extension of familial ties. Examples include adoption, also of adults, guardianship, fosterage, slavery and manumission. Demosthenes again offers a telling example in his Oration 36, *For Phormio.* (This was a different Phormio than the one accused in Oration 34, above). Phormio had used to be a slave and worked in the banking business of his master. He was manumitted, and upon the death of his former master he married the widow. He had acted as guardian of his former masters' property and his two minor sons and had even been awarded Athenian citizenship. While this was hardly the typical career of a slave, Phormio nevertheless enters into a series of legal positions of highly different status within the household of his former master. Extension of households for shorter or longer periods of time could also take place by the institution of *xenia,* that is guest-friendship. As Herman argues this institution invariably connected people belonging to different social units, and it entailed very real demands on reciprocal behavior, including trust and protection (Herman, 2002). Examples of how this might have worked in practice might be seen in the New Testament *Acts,* where Paul in the course of his travels stays with members of the local Jewish communities, sometimes over prolonged periods of time, and this gives him access to speak in the local synagogue. Jewish networks are well attested in the Medieval Indian Ocean (Goitein & Friedman, 2008; Margariti, 2007), and there is reason to believe that they were already established by the early first millennium CE (Seland, 2012, 2013, 2016).

On a societal level many ancient communities had laws regulating the rights of foreigners. While compared to modern times these would often appear discriminatory, they were in fact a way of including foreigners into the community and thereby offering them protection (Herman, 2002), thus making transactions possible. Plato describes legislation concerning the reception and protection of merchants to be a necessary part of the laws of a city state (*Laws* 12.952e–953a). Traces of treaties or laws regulating and protecting visitors from abroad are probably evident in the labeling of certain markets in the Indian Ocean as "legal"—*nomimon* in the *Periplus of the Erythraean Sea* (Rougé, 1987; Seland, 2022).

There is overlap between households and membership in groups based on communal, geographical or ethnical identity that seem to have been an important variable in distinguishing between *us* and *them* in cross-cultural exchanges in the ancient world. Greek texts were produced in the wider context of the imagined community, the *koinê,* of Greek-speakers, even if they, like Demosthenes' speeches, were intended for a specific audiences and occasions. Several of Demosthenes' forensic orations involve people who were not born in Athens or who were resident aliens. While Athenians are frequently identified by patronym or their membership in the civic unit of a *deme,* non-Athenian Greeks are generally identified with the city they came from. The much less numerous non-Greeks, on the other hand, are described with ethnicity, for instance Theodorus the Phoenician (Dem. *Or.* 34) and Pamphilus the Egyptian (Dem. *Or.* 35). Within the later framework of the Roman empire, associations of merchants and expatriates took geographical origin as their criterion of membership, such as the *collegia* in evidence across the Roman world (Harland, 2003, pp. 33–36), and the various *stationes* that existed in Puteoli and Ostia (Terpstra, 2013; Verboven, 2011). Merchants and soldiers from the Syrian city of Palmyra identified with their hometown whenever we encounter them in public settings abroad (Schörle, 2024), but obviously felt no need to do this when they were at home. In their case the identity might also be described as ethnic, as it was defined not only through origin and legal status, but also through shared cultural ties as expressed in language and religion, and to our knowledge membership was ascribed by being born into the community (Seland, 2013). Significantly Palmyrene Jews seem to have identified as Palmyrene whenever they were operating outside the city, while in Palmyra, in funerary settings, it is only their names that give reason to believe that they belonged to the Jewish community in addition to the commonwealth of Palmyrenes (Cussini, 2025).

The longstanding Sogdian network is also an example of a trading system based ultimately on ethnicity, with a Sogdian diaspora settled across Central Asia, household, local community and shared language and culture offered additional trust-creating institutions (de la Vaissière, 2005). In the western Indian Ocean, again on authority of the *Periplus of the Erythraean Sea*, but also drawing on Christian texts from Late Antiquity, traders and local populations were assigned to *etically*, that is externally constructed groups such as Greeks, Arabs, Persians, Indians, South Indians, Romans, Fish-Eaters (Ichtyophagoi) and nomads. These groups were identified on basis such as diet, language, dress, lifestyle and physical appearance (Seland, 2013). We have little or no information on what in-group or *emic* ties these communities maintained, nevertheless they might be described as based on ethnic identities as ancestry, whether real or imagined was the decisive factor in ascribing membership to different groups, and borders were maintained toward other communities. This does not necessarily imply that people described as Greek shared actual Greek ancestry in the sense that their ancestors actually had lived in Greece at some time. As Jonathan Hall has argued, Greek identity in Egypt by this time was defined by language and culture rather than descent (Hall, 2002). We are dealing with imagined communities both when adopting etic and emic perspectives.

An institution partly overlapping with ethnicity is that of religion. Landa emphasizes how religion lowers transaction costs between fellow believers by introducing shared ties, such as beliefs, worldview and worship, while at the same time imposing membership costs, such as marriage restrictions, dietary laws and other rules about purity, that make it easier to interact within the group than with outsiders (1994, pp. 131–134). Historian of religion Jonathan Z. Smith distinguished between religion "here," religion "there" and religion "anywhere." By religion here he described worship taking place within the primary social group, usually the household. By religion there, he referred to worship in the temple or another physical location and within a close community such as the tribe or city state. By religion anywhere, he denoted worship that took place independent of primary social group and location (Smith, 2004). The latter kind of religion, dubbed "portable" by historian William McNeill (McNeill, 1987), included Buddhism, Judaism, Christianity, Manichaeism, Hinduism, Jainism, Zoroastrianism and later Islam, which, albeit to different degrees in different places and periods of their history, were at least open to or in several cases actively encouraged proselytization. These were important in creating open-access in-groups that reached across communal divisions based on ethnicity, citizenship, caste and similar institutions. The evidence for religion as an institution underpinning trade networks is ample, ranging from Buddhism, Manichaeism and Christianity in Central Asia to Judaism, Christianity and later Islam in the Indian Ocean, and onwards to protestant entrepreneurial networks in the modern world (Foltz, 1999; Landa, 1994, pp. 131–134; Ray, 1998; Ray, 2024; Seland, 2013, 2014). The traditional faiths that these religions competed with, "religion there," were in general connected to group and place. The Bel of Palmyra, the chief god of the Palmyrene pantheon, was primarily a god for Palmyra and the Palmyrenes. Nevertheless, people from outside would also come to his temple and worship, as evident from the inscriptions they left there, and gods like Mithras and Jupiter Dolichenus were worshiped across the Roman Empire. Sanctuaries served as access points, where outsiders would come to ask for divine protection, thereby also establishing connection with local social networks (Seland, 2012). At the Egyptian Red Sea port of Berenike, inscriptions and objects reveal that worshippers from not only Egypt and the Mediterranean world, but also from the Horn of Africa, South Arabia, South Asia, all came to worship at the temple dedicated to Isis, an Egyptian goddess associated with the protecting of seafarers, over a period spanning close to five centuries (Sidebotham, 2014; Sidebotham et al., 2023). The inscriptions from the Hoq-cave, discussed in Chapter 2, revealing worshippers of Buddhist and Brahminic leanings (Strauch, 2012), is an interesting example of adherents of so-called portable faiths transposing their worship to a location with localized religious significance, cf. Abgar the Palmyrenes invocation of "the gods of the cave." As Himanshu P. Ray has demonstrated, the Berenike Isis-temple and the cave-sanctuary at Hoq are by far not the only sacred spaces in the Indian Ocean world with such evidence of religious polyphony, underlining that although religious texts tend to emphasize competition and exclusivity, the religious landscapes seascapes of the Indian Ocean world as seen from the perspective of worshippers, were in fact fluid and flexible (Ray, 2024).

Association and religion were intimately linked, as associations invariably had worship at the core of their justification and activity (Gabrielsen, 2007; Harland, 2003). In South Asian Brahmanistic traditions membership in a profession would follow *jāti* (caste) as ascribed by birth. While many associations were formed by people with common geographical or ethnic background, others regulated access according to profession, including that of merchants. Voluntary associations were ubiquitous in the ancient world, and by no means a phenomenon restricted to the Mediterranean. Associations of tradesmen and traders as an embedded part of Indian societal fabric and the existence of guilds, (*śreṇis*) are well attested both from normative texts such as the Arthashastra and from epigraphic and literary sources, and were often aligned with Buddhist monastic orders (*sanghas*) (Chandra, 1977; Evers, 2017; Ray, 1986; Trautmann, 2023). Associations also remind us that the social networks interconnecting the ancient world were to a large extent urban networks. These associations were based in cities, they operated with the permission of city-authorities. They took part in the civic life of cities, and known statues of associations are even based on the template of the city, with elected magistrates leading and representing the association (Wojciechowski, 2021).

The range of institutions facilitating trust within and between social networks in the ancient world resemble those that Landa identified in her model of the Ethnically Homogenous Middlemen Group. As outlined above, Landa operated with a seven-level hierarchy in her analysis of the Hokkien community of modern (1994, Wickström & Landa, 2018). While we should not expect an exact match with the ancient evidence, and neither that all ancient exchange networks would follow the same logic, there are nevertheless functional similarities that may be observed. Dealing with family and household members, as was the case in several of the cited examples from the Greek world, might correspond to the near kin category (1) of Landa. Greek phratries and Palmyrene lineages, to mention two examples, have parallels to distant kin (2) in the model. Clansmen and fellow villagers among the Hokkien (4) resemble members of both ancestry-based and civic tribes in the Greek and Roman worlds and have elements in common with profession/ancestry-based *jātis* (3). Associations based on profession or origin has some of the same role. City state or national identity, for instance as Sogdian, Palmyrene, Athenian, or, in the case of South Asian visitors to Socotra, *Yavana,* would correspond to the modern community of fellow Hokkiens (5), while broad cultural identities such as Greek, Roman, Indian, Persian correspond to the common Chinese identity (6).

Paul's use of social networks in the New Testament *Acts* may serve as a case in point. Paul and his companions travel from city to city, staying with local Jews and speaking in the local synagogue, thereby making use of the possibilities offered by being invited to temporarily join a household and the ethnoreligious network of Jewish places of worship. In one case he associates with a fellow tent-maker (*Acts* 18.1–3), and goes into business with him, drawing on professional ties. Much of his first missionary work takes place among the so-called "God-fearers," gentiles attending the synagogue and interested in Jewish religion, but not ready to pay the cost of actually joining the club, including circumcision and dietary restrictions (Stark, 2012, pp. 76–84). In a few cases when situations escalated, he was able to draw on his legal status as Roman citizen, for instance in order to get out of jail (*Acts* 16.37). While Paul was not a merchant, he operated within the same social infrastructure that constituted the commercial networks of the period.

The challenge remained of creating trust between business partners in cases when shared ties were lacking (7). Reputation, hospitality, friendship, marriage, pseudo-kinship and religion were some of the institutions that could create or such ties. In addition, came the existence of legislation, treaties. and other institutions regulating and protecting the rights of aliens. Ancient trading networks were by nature social networks and social networks were part of urban networks. The added value of combining social ties with commercial relations was that it provided ways to establish trust, thereby reducing transaction costs, on the other hand, it increased the cost of breaking contract, as breach of trust would inflict loss of standing within your social group.

References

Anderson, B. (1991). *Imagined communities: Reflections on the origin and spread of nationalism*. Verso.

Aslanian, S. D. (2011). *From the Indian Ocean to the Mediterranean: The global trade networks of Armenian merchants from New Julfa*. University of California Press.

Bang, P. F. (2008). *The Roman bazaar: A comparative study of trade and markets in a tributary empire*. Cambridge University Press.
Barth, F. (1969). Introduction. In F. Barth (Ed.), *Ethnic groups and boundaries: The social organization of cultural difference* (pp. 9–38). Universitetsforlaget.
Brubaker, R. (2002). Ethnicity without groups. *Archives Européennes de Sociologie, 43*(2), 163–189.
Chandra, M. (1977). *Trade routes in Ancient India*. Abhinav Publications.
Cohen, A. (1971). Cultural strategies in the organization of trading diasporas. In C. Meillassoux (Ed.), *The development of indigenous trade and markets in West Africa* (pp. 266–284). Oxford University Press.
Conceicao, J. L. (2016). Hokkien community. In *Singapore Infopedia. An electronic encyclopedia on Singapore's history, culture, people and events*. National Library Board. https://www.nlb.gov.sg/main/article-detail?cmsuuid=4fd3409a-79c9-4b3e-85e4-e321f764f91f [01.07.2025].
Curtin, P. D. (1984). *Cross cultural trade in world history*. Cambridge University Press.
Cussini, E. (2025). Mobility and identity of Palmyrene Jews. In R. Raja (Ed.), *Palmyra, the Mediterranean and beyond* (pp. 187–211). Cambridge University Press.
de la Vaissière, É. (2005). *Sogdian traders: A History*. Brill.
Dercksen, J. D. (2014). The Old Assyrian trade and its participants. In H. D. Baker & M. Jursa (Eds.), *Documentary sources in ancient Near Eastern and Greco-Roman economic history. Methodology and practice* (pp. 59–112). Oxbow Books.
Droß-Krüpe, K., Ruffing, K., & Föllinger, S. (2016). *Antike Wirtschaft und ihre kulturelle Prägung*. Harrassowitz Verlag.
Endreß, M. (2023). Vertrauen – Historische Filiationen, aktuelle Konstellationen, systematische Explikationen. In P. Reinard & C. Rollinger (Eds.), *Cum magna fide? Vertrauen und die antike Wirtschaft / Trust and the Ancient Economy* (pp. 37–56). Scripta Mercaturae Verlag.
Evers, K. G. (2011). *'With a little help from my friends'—A New Institutional Economics approach to the ancient economy*. University of Copenhagen.
Evers, K. G. (2017). *Worlds apart trading together: The organisation of long-distance trade between Rome and India in antiquity*. Archaeopress.
Foltz, R. C. (1999). *Religions of the silk road: Overland trade and cultural exchange from antiquity to the fifteenth century*. Macmillan.
Gabrielsen, V. (2007). Brotherhoods of faith and provident planning: The Non-public associations of the Greek world. *Mediterranean Historical Review, 22*(2), 183–210.
Geertz, C. (1978). The bazaar economy: Information and search in peasant marketing. *The American Economic Review, 68*(2), 28–32.

Goitein, S. D., & Friedman, M. A. (2008). *India traders of the Middle Ages: Documents from the Cairo Geniza: India book*. Brill.

Graeber, D., & Wengrow, D. (2021). *The dawn of everything: A new history of humanity*. Farrar.

Hall, J. M. (2002). *Hellenicity: Between ethnicity and culture*. University of Chicago Press.

Hammond, M. (Ed.). (2021). *The Peloponnesian war*. Oxford University Press.

Harari, Y. N. (2015). *Sapiens: A brief history of humankind*. Harper.

Harland, P. A. (2003). *Associations, synagogues, and congregations: Claiming a place in ancient Mediterranean society*. Fortress.

Herman, G. (2002). *Ritualised friendship and the Greek city*. Cambridge University Press.

Hobbes, T. (1651). *Leviathan, or the matter, forme, & power of a common-wealth, ecclesiasticall and civill*. Andrew Crooke.

Jones, N. F. (1999). *The associations of classical Athens: The response to democracy*. Oxford University Press.

Klosko, G., & Rice, D. (1985). Thucydides and Hobbes's State of Nature. *History of Political Thought, 6*(3), 405–409.

Landa, J. T. (1994). *Trust, ethnicity, and identity: Beyond the New Institutional Economics of ethnic trading networks, contract Law, and gift-exchange*. University of Michigan Press.

Larsen, M. T. (2000). The Old Assyrian city-state. In M. H. Hansen (Ed.), *A comparative study of thirty city-state cultures: An investigation conducted by the Copenhagen Polis Centre* (pp. 77–87). Det Kongelige Danske Videnskabernes Selskab.

Manger, L. O. (2010). *The Hadrami diaspora: Community-building on the Indian Ocean rim*. Berghahn Books.

Margariti, R. E. (2007). *Aden & the Indian Ocean trade: 150 years in the life of a medieval Arabian port*. University of North Carolina Press.

McNeill, W. (1987). The era of civilizations in world history. *Newsletter of the World History Association, 4*(1), 1–4.

North, D. C. (1990). *Institutions, institutional change and economic performance*. Cambridge University Press.

North, D. C., Wallis, J. J., & Weingast, B. R. (2009). *Violence and social orders: A conceptual framework for interpreting recorded human history*. Cambridge University Press.

Posner, R. A. (1980). A theory of primitive society, with special reference to law. *The Journal of Law and Economics, 23*(1), 1–53.

Ray, H. P. (1986). *Monastery and guild: Commerce under the Satavahanas*. Oxford University Press.

Ray, H. P. (1998). *The winds of change—Buddhism and the maritime Links of early South Asia*. Oxford University Press.

Ray, H. P. (2024). Religious networks, coastal temples, and heritage routes of the Indian Ocean World. *Acta via Serica, 9*(2), 85–109.

Reinard, P., & Rollinger, C. (Eds.). (2023). *Cum magna fide?* Scripta Mercaturae Verlag.

Rougé, J. (1987). "Emporion Nomimon". Recherches sur la terminologie du Périple de la mer Erythrée. *Index, 15*, 405–411.

Scheidel, W., Morris, I., & Saller, R. P. (2007). *The Cambridge economic history of the Greco-Roman world*. Cambridge University Press.

Schörle, K. (2024). The Palmyrene diaspora. In R. Raja (Ed.), *The Oxford handbook of Palmyra* (pp. 251–260).

Seland, E. H. (2012). Trade and Christianity in the Indian Ocean during late antiquity. *Journal of Late Antiquity, 5*(1), 72–86.

Seland, E. H. (2013). Networks and social cohesion in ancient Indian Ocean trade: Geography, ethnicity, religion. *Journal of Global History, 8*(3), 373–390.

Seland, E. H. (2014). Early Christianity in East Africa and Red Sea/Indian Ocean commerce. *African Archaeological Review, 31*(4), 637–647.

Seland, E. H. (2016). Trade diasporas and merchant social cohesion in early trade in the Western Indian Ocean. In D. H. Akenson & A. Chowdhury (Eds.), *Between dispersion and belonging: Global approaches to diaspora in practice* (pp. 125–137). McGill-Queen's University Press.

Seland, E. H. (2022). Markets in the Erythra Thalassa. In K. Dross-Krüpe & K. Ruffing (Eds.), *Markt, Märkte und Marktgebäude in der antiken Welt* (pp. 393–402). Harrassowitz.

Seland, E. H. (2023a). Palmyra and the Indian Ocean. In S. Baumann, K. Droß-Krüpe, S. Fink, S. Günther, & P. Reinard (Eds.), *Trade and seafaring in antiquity. Red Sea – Persian Gulf – Indian Ocean* (pp. 227–240). Zaphon.

Seland, E. H. (2023b). Trust networks in ancient cross-cultural and long-distance trade. In P. Reinard & C. Rollinger (Eds.), *Cum magna fide? Vertrauen und die antike Wirtschaft / Trust and the Ancient Economy* (pp. 105–116). Scripta Mercaturae Verlag.

Seland, E. H. (2024). The Caravan families of Palmyra: Prosopographical evidence of elite Involvement in long-distance commerce. *Digital Classics Online, 10*(2). https://doi.org/10.11588/dco.2024.10.103976

Sidebotham, S. E. (2014). Religion and burial at the Ptolemaic-Roman Red Sea Emporium of Berenike, Egypt. In *African Archaeological Review 31*(4), pp. 599–635.

Sidebotham, S. E., Ast, R., Kaper, O. E., Bergmann, M., Bhandare, S., Maurer, A., … & Stoye, M. (2023). Results of the Winter 2022 excavation season at Berenike (Red Sea Coast), Egypt. *Thetis, 27*, 13–28.

Smith, J. Z. (2004). Here, there and anywhere. In J. Z. Smith (Ed.), *Relating religion: Essays in the study of religion* (pp. 323–338). Chicago University Press.

Stark, R. (2012). *The triumph of Christianity: How the Jesus movement became the world's largest religion*. Harper Collins.

Terpstra, T. T. (2013). *Trading communities in the Roman world: A micro-economic and institutional perspective*. Brill.

Trautmann, T. R. (2023). Forest people in the Kauṭilīya Arthaśāstra. In C. T. Fleming, T. L. Knudsen, A. Misra, & V. Sharma (Eds.), *Science and society in the Sanskrit World* (pp. 325–342). Brill.

Veenhof, K. R. (2013). The archives of Old Assyrian traders: Their nature, functions and use. In M. Faraguna (Ed.), *Archives and archival documents in Ancient Societies* (pp. 27–61). EUT Edizioni Università di Trieste.

Verboven, K. (2011). Resident aliens and translocal merchant collegia in the Roman Empire. In T. Kaizer & O. Hekster (Eds.), *Frontiers in the Roman world* (pp. 335–348). Brill.

von Reden, S., & Kowalzig, B. (2022). New Institutional Economics, economic growth, and institutional change. In S. von Reden (Ed.), *The Cambridge companion to the ancient Greek economy* (pp. 347–359). Cambridge University Press.

Wickström, B.-A., & Landa, J. T. (2018). Interethnic relations, informal trading networks, and social integration: Imitation, habits, and social evolution. *Journal of Bioeconomics, 20*(3), 263–286.

Wojciechowski, P. (2021). Ad exemplum rei publicae. *Klio. Czasopismo Poświęcone Dziejom Polski i Powszechnym, 58*(2), 133–143.

CHAPTER 4

Things

Abstract This chapter starts by explaining the concepts and implications of material agency and the so-called material turn in the social sciences. Bruno Latour's Actor-Network Theory is introduced, along with Ian Hodder's concept of entanglement as ways of applying these insights in practice. Then two examples follow. We trace the journey of a peppercorn from its harvest in the Western Ghat mountains in present-day Kerala to its consumers in a Roman military camp on the Wall of Hadrian. After this we visit gold- and silver mines in Roman Spain and follow coins on their journey to southern India, northwestern China and Scandinavia, discussing how these objects took on different significance as they changed hands along the road. The final part of the chapter discusses how objects formed networks of things when they were moved and exchanged, drawing on the lists of Indian Ocean trade goods preserved in the first century CE *Periplus of the Erythraean Sea*.

Keywords Material agency · Actor-Network-Theory · Entanglement · Pepper trade · Roman Coinage

© The Author(s), under exclusive license to Springer Nature Switzerland AG 2026
E. H. Seland, *Long-Distance Trade in the Ancient World*, Palgrave Studies in Ancient Economies,
https://doi.org/10.1007/978-3-031-90855-2_4

The narrative of J.R.R. Tolkien's fantasy epic, *The Lord of the Rings,* revolves around a golden ring, forged long ago by Sauron, the lord of darkness, in the lava streams deep below Mount Doom. The ring is supposed to grant Sauron control of the free peoples of Middle Earth—dwarves, elves and men. Sauron's plan fails and he loses the ring, which sets out on a journey from hand to hand, shaping the fate not only of its carriers, but also on those around them and the world at large, as the ring seeks to be reunited with its creator.

Tolkien had borrowed the motive of the ring, also central to Richard Wagner's epic musical drama, *The Ring of the Niebelung,* from Scandinavian and German mythology. These modern stories of a Ring of power were pieced together from a group of epic poems known as the Völsung cycle, written down in Iceland in the Medieval period, but building on older oral traditions that went back to the migration period of the mid-first millennium CE. In these poems the ring was first forged by the dwarf Andvari to help him find gold. When it was stolen by the god Loki, Andvari cursed the ring, setting off a chain of murder and misfortune among those that later came across it. The One ring thus possesses agency, which means potential to act. It touches the lives of everyone that encounters it (Hammer, 2018). Things in the real world are hardly that powerful. Nevertheless, they have agency, because they reach into our lives and because we invest them with meaning and value. Although of mythical nature, the story of Andvari's ring reminds us that people in the past were no different. The Germanic literary motif of the ring of power seems to have historical analogues in practices of rings being handed from rulers to retainers as symbols of relationships of fealty again emulating Roman military practices of using golden neck and arm rings as rewards for exceptional service (Skre, 2025, pp. 105, 190, 287–289).

That things matter is no new insight. A milestone of the so-called material turn in the social and human sciences was the 1986 volume, The Social Life of Things, where the authors argued precisely that people invest objects with value and meaning, and that, as this is a process that takes place through social interaction, objects have an important role in understanding the relations between people (Appadurai, 1986). Bruno Latour, through much of his work described how people, objects and their physical environment, man-made as well as natural, enter into endless chains of interactions, and thereby form networks that reach across space as well as time. In his Actor-Network Theory Objects assume the role of what Latour called actants rather than agents, to underline that agency does not necessarily imply intention or consciousness in bringing these connections about, but that objects are nevertheless instrumental in making things happen. One of Latour's examples is the car, consisting of thousands of components, assembled, and thus also connected in ways that make them work as what we most of the time consider a single unit. Most of these parts are critical for the safe operation of that unit, and does not only bring the car in connection with a number of surfaces as it moves around, but also us as passengers or drivers in contact with each other. (Latour, 2005)

Many historians and archaeologists have been inspired by Latour's insight, but have found it challenging to apply them on their material, as the number of possible connections between actants appears to be infinite. One attempt that has met with some success is that of Ian Hodder, who developed the concept of entanglement and the method of the tanglegram as a tool to explore the relationship between archaeological data. Hodder uses the tanglegram to map how the material of clay enters into contexts with other material, objects and environments, including ovens, clay pits, refuse heaps, reeds, marshes, animal bones, houses and so on, at the neolithic site of Çatalhüyük (Türkiye) prompting us to ask for the role of humans in bringing about these relations, and thus getting closer to understanding the significance of the material (Hodder, 2012). In this way, Hodder's tool also reminds us that objects are part of a wider material world. People in the ancient world knew no synthetic processes. Their tools, clothes, medical drugs and jewelry, although combined, mixed, processed, shaped, moved and manipulated in different ways, were extracted from the ground using muscular power of people and animals, made from animals who would often die in the process, or harvested from plants that would only grow under certain climatic conditions. While much of this remains true even today, tracing how these chains of operation played out gives insight into how humans interacted with and depended on their environment. In this chapter, we examine two cases of material mobility and entanglement across ancient Afro-Eurasia, pepper corns and precious metals, before discussing how objects formed networks with places, people and animals discussed in previous chapters.

The Journey of a Peppercorn

By the first century CE, black pepper had become all the rage in the Roman empire. Available in Roman army camps on the northern borders of Roman Britain and along the Danube, the tiny black grains were used in food, wine, medicine, cosmetics and magical potions (Cobb, 2018). Black pepper is mentioned hundreds of times in Apicus' famous book *On the Art of cooking* (*De re coquinara*). Pliny the elder gives the price of four denarii for a Roman lb of the Indian spice (328.9 grams), which almost amounts to the weekly pay of a Roman legionary of his days (Pliny, N.H. 12.28; Harl, 1996, pp. 216, 283). Pliny was horrified at the price, but anyone familiar with the South Asian spice knows that not much is needed to add flavor to your food. It is regularly sold today by the ounce or even in smaller units, and was likely available to a quite large segment of Roman consumers (Cobb, 2018). An apt analogy might be saffron, famous for being the most expensive spice available. Saffron today sells at c. USD 1000 per Roman lb, well above many weekly net salaries today, but few people need a Roman pound of saffron, and most consumers can afford the limited amounts they require whenever they think it is worthwhile in order to prepare a favorite dish. Nicholas Purcell, writing about frankincense, not pepper, labeled such commodities "unnecessary dependences," that is products that are somewhere between actual luxuries and basic needs (Purcell, 2016). Even at Rome's darkest hour, when Alaric and his army of Goths were at the gates of Rome in 409 CE, the ransom demanded for the city included 3000 pounds of pepper, along with 4000 silk robes, made from a commodity that had traveled even farther than the pepper. Within the three days set as a deadline, the ransom was collected by the senate from the citizens of Rome, who thereby bought themselves a brief peace with the Goths, who, however, came back to sack the city next year, possibly looking for more pepper (Zosimus, *Nea Historia*, 5.41).

Although it is now cultivated in many parts of the tropical world, the original habitat of pepper was limited to the region of Kerala in present-day South India, where it was extensively cultivated by the early centuries of the Common Era (Malekandasthil, 2016). A Tamil poem of the early historic period reports that 'great ships of the Yavanas arrive with gold and depart with pepper' (*Purunanuru* 343). As mentioned in chapters two and three, Yavana had originally held the meaning "Greek," but over time acquired the wider sense of foreigner (Zvelebil, 1956), and would likely refer to visitors from the Roman world, the Persian/Arabian Gulf, or northwest—India in this context. Other poems praise Tamil rulers, who consume and share the wine of the Yavanas (*Ahananuru* 149, *Purananuru* 56). A mural, likely of the fifth century CE, in the rock-cut Ajanta caves in Maharashtra depicts a Yavana, identifiable by headwear and facial hair, pouring wine from a glass goblet (Fig. 4.1), another prestigious Mediterranean import, as evident for instance in the finds of Roman glass in sealed storerooms of the first century CE excavated in Begram in present-day Afghanistan.

Mediterranean amphorae have been found in many locations along the Indian Coast (Tomber, 2007). Two sites stand out with respect to the archaeological record, Arikamedu near Pondicherry on the Coromandel Coast, and Pattanam in Kerala (Begley et al., 1996; Cherian, 2016; Tomber, 2016). These were centers of exchange, and thus nodes

Fig. 4.1 Yavana pouring wine. Sengai Podhuvan/Wikimedia Commons, CC BY-SA 3.0

in the urban networks of the period. Pattanam, called Muziris in ancient texts, was one of the places where ships from Egypt and Mesopotamia arrived to exchange wine and gold for pepper. Arikamedu served as a gateway settlement between the South Indian hinterland networks and the Bay of Bengal small-world system. South Indian ports were located in river estuaries, where bends in the river created safe anchorage for ocean-going ships, while the river facilitated communication with the hinterland by canoe or other rivercraft.

Pepper is a climber, which grows as a parasite on trees. It is harvested between January and March and dried outdoors. Black, white and green pepper are all products of the same plant treated differently. Harvesting and drying are work that does not require much in terms of training or central organization. Finished products would be transported to the coast by carriers, buffaloes and riverboats, well before the summer monsoon rains start in June, which would make roads difficult and cargo vulnerable to humidity. Pepper was then gathered and stored in the coastal center of Muziris, for much of the early historical period controlled by rulers of the Tamil Chera dynasty, the rulers of one of three polities competing for control of South India. Ships from the Mediterranean would arrive here in September, but not leave again before January, because of the wind regimes in the Arabian Sea and southern Red Sea (Casson, 1989, pp. 297–299; Seland, 2016b, p. 56). Ships with crews from South India also took part in the trade, following the same seasonal pattern, as ceramics, graffiti, a bilingual Sanskrit-Greek inscription dated to the mid-third century CE, and a statue of the Buddha dated to the second century CE, all from the Egyptian Red Sea port of Berenike document (Begley & Tomber, 1999; Sidebotham, 2011, pp. 74–75; Sidebotham et al., 2023).

Literary texts mention different varieties of ships built in Arabia, South Asian and African traditions of shipbuilding (cf. Blue, 2009). Archaeological remains reveal that some vessels were of the kind common in the Mediterranean, assembled in shipyards on the Red Sea, built by wood from Lebanon or the Balkan peninsula, using shell first and mortise and tenon technique. Repairs made in Indian wood as well as use of Indian cotton sails are archaeologically attested from ports in Egypt (Blue et al., 2011; Sidebotham, 2008; Whitewright, 2007). Pepper would probably be shipped in jars to keep the cargo dry. At the Berenike, a large South Asian storage jar (*dolium*) was excavated in the courtyard of the Isis temple, still containing its cargo of 7,55 kilogram of black pepper (Cappers, 2006, pp. 114–119). Such jars appear too bulky and heavy for overland transport, and goods were likely repacked for onwards shipping several times during their journey from India to Roman consumers. It is not possible to say whether the pepper was a gift to the temple from seafarers grateful for safe passage, or if its location indicates that the temple was involved in trade, but in either case its presence at Berenike show that pepper was also consumed by the people who were active in trade and transport (Sidebotham, 2014, pp. 615).

Ships from India would arrive in Berenike in February or March (Casson, 1989, pp. 283–291; Seland, 2016b, p. 56). A papyrus from the second century CE containing details about the transit and taxation of a shipment from Muziris, very likely containing a large amount of pepper (De Romanis, 2012), seems to indicate that goods would be inspected upon arrival in Egypt, then, whatever was not destined for Berenike itself, like the dolium of pepper just mentioned, was sealed and transported to Alexandria by way of the Nile-port of Koptos (Rathbone, 2000). The transit from Berenike on the Red Sea coast to Koptos took about twelve days, along roads maintained and policed by Roman authorities in return for quite heavy tolls documented in an inscription called the Koptos tariff (Adams, 2007, pp. 37–41, 132–133). When goods arrived at the Nile, the water level was low and river traffic was only possible with small boats (Cooper, 2008). Thus, the goods were placed in public warehouses in Koptos, awaiting the July–August Nile flood, which would make navigation toward Alexandria easier again. In Alexandria, there was also a designated warehouse for the collection of the special 25% tax on eastern imports, and after that we must assume that the rest of the goods were at the disposal of the owner (Seland, 2011). The Mediterranean sailing season ended in October, and goods destined for the imperial market might or might not have to wait until next spring before they were transported toward Rome by ships heading first north to Crete or Anatolia, and then east to Italy, a journey of about a month (Casson, 1995). In Ostia, the harbor city of Rome, the pepper would be unloaded, transferred to riverboats, which were then tugged up to Rome along the river, another three days' journey (Malmberg, 2015). In Rome in the late first and second centuries, spices were stored and sold from special public warehouses called the *horrea piperataria*, indicating, that the tax on eastern imports was levied in kind, making the state a major agent in the spice trade (Loane, 1944). The warehouses were prominently situated along the Via *sacra*, the street leading to the Forum of Rome, which seems to have been a the place to go for spices, aromatics and other eastern imports in the imperial capital, A nearby street was revealingly known as the *vicus unguentarius* ("street of the perfumemakers") (Holleran, 2012, pp. 54, 246).

For the pepper to continue its journey to the soldiers stationed at the northern borders of the Roman empire would require a journey of at least another month of effective travel time. A possible route would be downriver or by boat back to Ostia at the mouth of the Tiber, by ship to Narbo (Narbonne), then onwards to Burdigala/Bordeaux by riverboat, again by ship to Durnovaria (Dorchester), before a coastal journey up the east coast of Britannia and a final haul along Hadrian's wall. Transhipment, waiting for beneficial winds or available transport, and bureaucratic red tape, would easily double the time, meaning that the peppercorns had spent a minimum of c. two years and covered approximately 12 000 kilometers from producer in South India to consumer in northern Britannia. Black pepper was not only enjoyed in the Roman empire. It is also documented as a commodity in Sogdian caravan trade with China by way of the Tarim Basin in the fourth century CE (de la Vaissière, 2005, pp. 53–54), and must have reached Central Asia by way of the routes described in the previous chapter, thus making it a truly global commodity within the first millennium world system.

The journey of peppercorns illustrates two points. The first is that connectivity in the ancient world was wrought with friction. It never took place in a single process or one stable and smooth movement. Pepper and other commodities made their way through the macro-network of the Afro-Eurasian world, passing through series of nodes, often cities, along their way, changing mode of transport at the intersection of regional networks, and coming into contact with people, animals, carriages, ships and so on as they moved along, thus actually being in possession of the kind of non-human agency surmised by Appadurai and colleagues in *The Social Life of Things* (1986). In the sense of Actor-Network Theory of Latour or material entanglement as conceived by Hodder, traveling commodities spun their own networks, reaching from the dense forests in the foothills of Kerala to the moors of Northumberland in Northern England, from there across time to modern scholarship and into this text. They brought into contact not only places and people, but also relied on the muscular power of buffaloes, camels, donkeys and mules, that belonged to and were handled by people, who thus in turn also became part of the social networks wrought by things (Chapter 5).

These networks depended on technology and infrastructure, including containers of textile, wood, leather and pottery; and ships made out of thousands of individually fitted pieces of wood, metal and fiber.

Money Makes the World Go Round

While we have a fair amount of knowledge about the process that brought pepper halfway across the ancient world, we know less about what significance it took on in the lives of people who were involved in the process, despite the grains of information contained in Roman and Tamil texts. An example of how objects take on different significance as they are invested with meaning in different contexts might, however, be found one of the main objects of exchange used by the Roman side in the pepper trade, namely coins.

Precious metals played a big part in long-distance trade in the Roman period. They are scarce, durable, and have a high value to weight ratio. Thus, they made attractive commodities and were easy to transport and store compared for instance to pepper. Gold and silver were extracted in many regions of the Roman empire, the most important mines in the first two centuries CE, that is the time of the *Periplus of the Erythraean Sea* and the Muziris papyrus, being in the Iberian Peninsula (Butcher, 2020). Mines were owned by the state and organized as leases, managed by contractors, who would use a mixed workforce of free labor, condemned criminals and slaves for the actual extraction and processing of ores, which, if the written sources are to be trusted, was extremely hard and dangerous work (Holleran, 2016). Mining was a huge industry, to the extent that traces of the lead pollution released by silver production can be traced in ice-cores from Greenland and used as proxy for Roman economic activity (McConnell et al., 2018). Bullion was coined in regional mints, often in the provincial capital, in the standard weight and shape of the Roman *denarius* for silver and *aureus* for gold, with the image of the Roman emperor as a guarantee of value. In most cases coinage was recalled when a new emperor took over, and in return for a modest fee exchanged with issues with the image of the new emperor (Butcher, 2020; Rolnick et al., 1997). For a long time Roman *denarii* had a very high silver content, but in 64 CE, Nero (ruled 54–68 CE) reduced the silver content, first to 80%, before backtracking to 90%. After Nero most new emperors followed his example, until Trajan (ruled 97–117) fixed the denarius at 80% silver in 100 CE (Butcher & Ponting, 2014, pp. 434–460). The next major debasement to 45% occurred during the rule of Septimius Severus (194–211), while the aureus remained almost pure gold until Caracallạ (ruled 211–217) (Murphy, 2020).

While new issues with lower precious-metal content seem to have been met with some distrust and there were many attempts at tuning (Butcher, 2020), it is also clear that there was a substantial element of trust in the system. Until the collapse in money-value during the civil war period of the third century CE, when competing emperors minted coins with as little as c. 2% silver in order to pay their troops, the denarius worked partly as a fiat currency, that is money with no intrinsic value, not unlike the banknotes that were standard until recently and that are still in use today. Other monetary systems in the ancient world depended on trust (and control) to an even greater extent. The Egyptian Ptolemaic coinage was kept on as a closed monetary system by the Romans after their takeover in Egypt, where coinage with near no silver or gold circulated for centuries (Christiansen, 1987). In Han-China, as in many Chinese states even earlier, coins of copper, bronze and iron were legal tender with higher face value than metal value. Supplemented by bullion the system relied on a combination of trust and government authority (Scheidel, 2010).

Beyond the reach of such politically based systems, however, things became more complicated. Trade with pepper for a large part took place by way of Egypt. Recipients of payments within Roman Egypt may well have been forced to accept debased official currency, but Egyptian coinage was all but worthless outside the province. In order to buy pepper from South India Roman traders needed to use coins with a high silver content, which have shown up by the thousands in South India (Turner, 1989). This happened immediately after Nero debased the coinage. This has sometimes been taken to estimate fluctuations in the value of trade with India, but hoards containing mainly high silver content coins of Augustus and Trajan, but including issues of Vespasian, Domitian, Trajan, Hadrian, Commodus and Antoninus Pius show that this was not the case (MacDowell, 2004). As these hoards were not deposited before the date of their youngest coin, they either circulated for a long time in India, or old coins were selected for the India-trade long after they ceased to circulate in the Roman empire (Mitchiner, 2004; Shastri, 2004). Unsurprisingly the number of Roman gold hoards in India increase after Nero's debasement of the silver currency. Experienced coin users could easily determine the pureness of alloys by weighing, heating or scratching coins

(Butcher, 2020, p. 10). As soon as the silver content of the denarii was reduced, South Asian sellers would prefer older issues, still circulating along the new ones for a long time in the Roman world, or switch to the still pure gold aurei. Roman buyers would adapt to this and collect old issues for trade with South India (Turner, 1989).

Local coinage in Tamil South India consisted of small, punch-marked coins of copper and silver (Hall, 1999; Majumdar, 2016, pp. 399–404). These were likely not used for everyday, smallscale transactions, but played a role in intra-elite, redistributive transactions and in the major centers of political power and long-distance exchange (Majumdar, 2016, pp. 395–396). While the punch-mark would presumably vouch for the metal purity and the issuing authority, coins vary in weight and would likely be weighed for transactions. This is probably part of the reason that so many Roman coins have survived in Southern India compared to states in Arabia, and North-India, which had their own silver-based systems (Mitchiner, 1976; Shastri, 2004), and likely melted down imported coins and struck new ones. Instead, in South India, Roman coins took on other uses. Roman coins probably circulated as money supplementing the local bullion-based systems (Majumdar, 2016; Shastri, 2004), especially within the South Indian elite and in high-value commercial transactions. However, they were also imitated by local rulers (Majumdar, 2016, pp. 408–411, 421–422), and also used as charms or jewelery, as specimens pierced for wearing indicate, and they served as patterns for terracotta bullae, showing that they were invested with prestige and symbolic power (Turner, 1989). Roman coins, in addition to their original function as means of payment in long-distance trade, and their regional role in the South Indian economy, also along with their imitations, thus seem to have become objects signifying wealth and good fortune that were disconnected from their value as money as well as metal, and thus functioned quite differently in the South Indian social setting than in the one that have produced them (Smagur, 2018).

The Indian example is not unique. While finds of Roman coins are exceedingly rare in China, some did end up there (Li, 2015). In Ningxia in northern China, five Byzantine gold coins from the fifth and sixth centuries were found in the tomb of a nobleman who died in 575 CE. Four of them were pierced for hanging, one of them was found in the mouth of the skeleton, likely analogue to the coeval Mediterranean custom of providing payment for the passage to the afterlife. Probably these coins also started their journey eastwards either as soldiers' pay or as payment for trade goods, but underway they took on different significance to their new owners. Roman coins also left the empire in other directions and by other mechanisms. C. 140 000 silver *denarii* have been found outside the Roman borders in central, northern and eastern Europe, c.12 500 of them in Scandinavia. The numbers obviously only represent a tiny fraction of those that were once exported (Bursche, 2002; Skre, 2025, p. 136). Coins certainly traveled for several reasons. But as most of the Roman silver money left the empire in the span of a few decades at the end of the second and start of the third century CE (Skre, 2025, pp. 136–137), their use as payment in trade, the most likely reason for coin export to India seems implausible. Along with the geopolitical context, the Marcomannic wars 166–180 CE and the peace settlements that followed it, it seems more likely that coins were exported either as subsidies to Germanic tribes (Bursche, 2002), or as payment to Germanic auxiliary soldiers in Roman service (Skre, 2025, pp. 170–172). Dagfinn Skre, in a recent study of the Scandinavian finds, holds the payment option to be the most likely for that group. He argues that Scandinavian warrior elites, after leaving Roman service as mercenaries, brought the coins home, where they were hoarded for later purposes, including payments to Roman traders, later return to the Roman empire, blood-money, dowries, payments to retainers, and other transactions within this elite sphere (2025, pp. 149–157).

While the influx of Roman silver coins to northern Europe all but stopped with the sharp decline in silver content in the third century, Roman gold money continued to leave the empire as payment and gifts to soldiers and allies. Analogous with the Indian situation they were also used for ornamental purposes, pierced or mounted for wearing, and imitated and providing inspiration for gold medallions known as bracteates, and commonly taken to be originally inspired by Roman models given to soldiers for long or exceptional service (Juliano et al., 2001, pp. 271–290; Skre, 2025, pp.459–478). Some 1167 such locally produced gold medallions, inspired by Roman patterns, struck by 725 dies, have been found, dating to the period c. 450–540 C.E (Skre, 2025, pp. 461–462). Many bracteates are believed to depict mythical scenes similar and related to those of the Germanic myths discussed at the outset of this chapter (Axboe, 2004). An alternative interpretation is that they were used as gifts from lords to their retainers, inspired with Roman practices (Skre, 2025, pp. 469–471) and partly analogous to the sociopolitical and redistributive role ascribed to Roman coins and their imitations in South India (Majumdar, 2016, pp. 421–422) (Figs. 4.2 and 4.3).

Fig. 4.2 Gold Aureus of Nero, 66–67 CE, obverse, Metropolitan Museum, Public Domain

Fig. 4.3 Gold bracteate showing a man wearing a helmet and a four-legged, horned animal. Museum of Cultural History, University of Oslo, CC BY 4.0. SA

Networks of Things

Network analytical tools make it possible to describe, visualize and analyze the networks created as objects move from place to place or change hands. A case in point is the *Periplus of the Erythraean Sea,* discussed above (Chapter 2). While the text describes trade and navigation in the Indian Ocean from the perspective of Roman Egypt, it also gives much information on South Asian, Arabian and African merchants and navigators, as their activities are portrayed in the passages describing the different ports visited by ships from Egypt. On a superficial level, the *Periplus* describes connections between ports in the Indian Ocean along with connections between adjacent ports (Fig. 2.5). This was a network of places, but also of people, as these connections existed only because and when people actually moved. We may, however, also read the *Periplus* as a network of things (Fig. 4.4; Seland, 2016c). While things obviously depended on people to move, they could change hands many times before they arrived at their destination, and their movement may serve as a proxy for the movement of people.

The entire network might be difficult to grasp, even if it might give an impression of the relative centrality of certain ports and commodities, but wine may serve as a case in point (Fig. 4.5). The *Periplus* (sec. 7–8) informs us that among other things, there was a market for wine from the Roman empire in the port of Malaô, present-day Berbera in northern Somaliland. The text also, however, lists a number of other ports that deal in wine, either as exporters or importers of the commodity. While the text describes trade in wine from Roman Egypt to Malaô, it also mentions several other regions that export wine including South Arabia and ports in the Persian/Arabian Gulf. In this manner we may also hypothesize contacts that are not mentioned in the text. Traders in Malaô in present-day Somaliland for instance might also have gotten the wine they wanted from other places than Egypt. The usefulness of this lies in formulating research questions that might be tested against other kinds of evidence. Fragments of South Arabian and Mesopotamian transport jars that cover a far longer period than the snapshot provided by the *Periplus* and the archaeological record of imports from the Mediterranean in Somaliland indicate that wine arrived here also from other parts of the western Indian Ocean (Seland, 2014). That the inhabitants of first century CE Malaô were fond of wine does not necessarily imply that they were still thirsty by the fourth or sixth century CE, but it provides basis

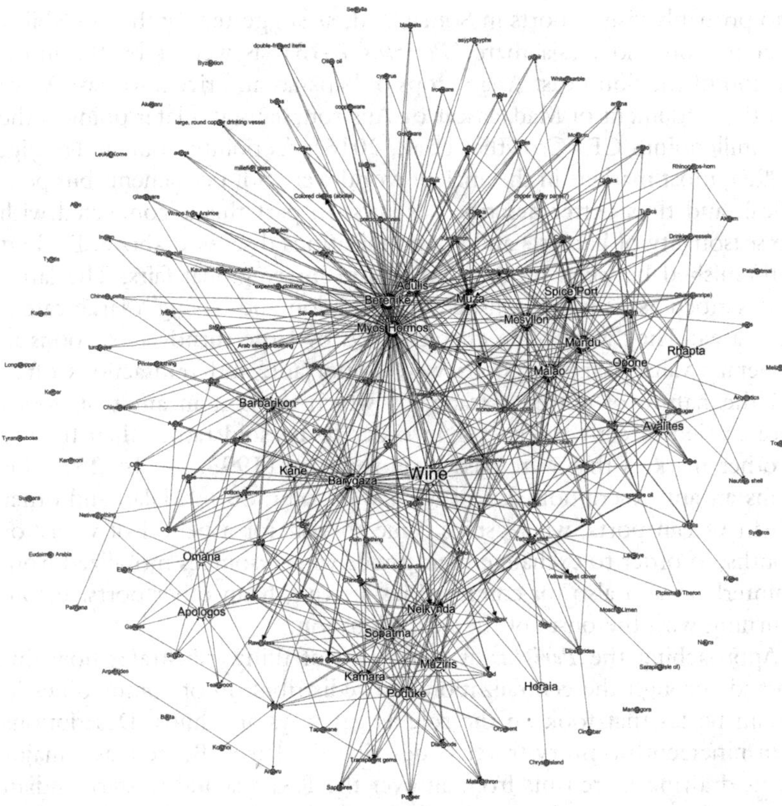

Fig. 4.4 The *Periplus Maris Erythraei* as a network of connections between places and products. Arrows indicate import or export. Labels and nodes are sized according to the number of mentions they receive in the text, indicating their centrality in the exchange networks CC BY 4.0 SA

for the hypothesis that the later transport jars may also have contained wine. Ports in Somaliland, which were visited by merchants not only from the Mediterranean, but also from South Arabia, northwestern India and South India, probably even from present-day Indonesia, and of course also from the African hinterland, would work as transit harbors or hubs. Although thus far only two fragments of Roman amphorae are reported from Thailand (Hoppál et al., 2023), wine was among the Mediterranean products that would be of interest to the merchants from Southeast Asia who probably visited ports in Somaliland, as suggested by the availability of cinnamon and cassia there (*Periplus* 7–13), as well as by the introduction of the Southeast-Asian crops of bananas and rice into East Africa and the settlement of Madagascar by Austronesians at a later point in the first millennium CE (Crowther et al., 2016). As pointed out by De Ligt (1993), most markets in the ancient world were not permanent, but periodical, and thus better described as fairs. In part this is connected with the seasonality of harvests and communications discussed above. De Ligt distinguished between local, regional and interregional fairs. The latter he described as being of considerable duration and having a large catchment area. They were often characterized by large turnover of goods in monetary value. Luxury goods were important, and transactions often had the nature of entrepôt trade, by which de Ligt meant that goods were carried directly to the fair in order to be sold rather than by way of other markets that were passed on the road (1993, pp. 14–25). This seems an apt description also of what was going on in Malaô and other Indian Ocean ports, where ships came to visit for a period of weeks or months, in order to exchange their goods with resources mobilized from a hinterland and also for commodities arriving from other ports, before returning with the onset of the next monsoon.

Approaching the *Periplus* as a network of things illustrates how this worked through the centralization and redistribution of commodities in certain places that took on the role as gateways and hubs. Descriptions from nineteenth-century travelers describe the fair at Berbera as a major event, drawing merchants from all over the Red Sea and western Indian Ocean, along with a thousands of hinterland residents for a few hectic winter months (e.g., Cruttenden, 1849). Even without assuming any kind of continuity such descriptions allow us to better envision what was going on in the ancient period.

A different category of products that figures prominently in the *Periplus* is textiles (Seland, 2016a). Textiles are interesting, because unlike aromatics and gemstones, that moved not only, but nevertheless mainly from South Asia toward the Mediterranean, textiles appear to be moving in all directions. Silk, as described in the *Periplus,* originated in China. It reached the Indian Ocean network by two itineraries, either by way of Central Asia and down the Indus to ports on the west coast of the Indian subcontinent, or through the small-world networks or trading circuits of the East China Sea and the Bay of Bengal. From Indian ports, however it

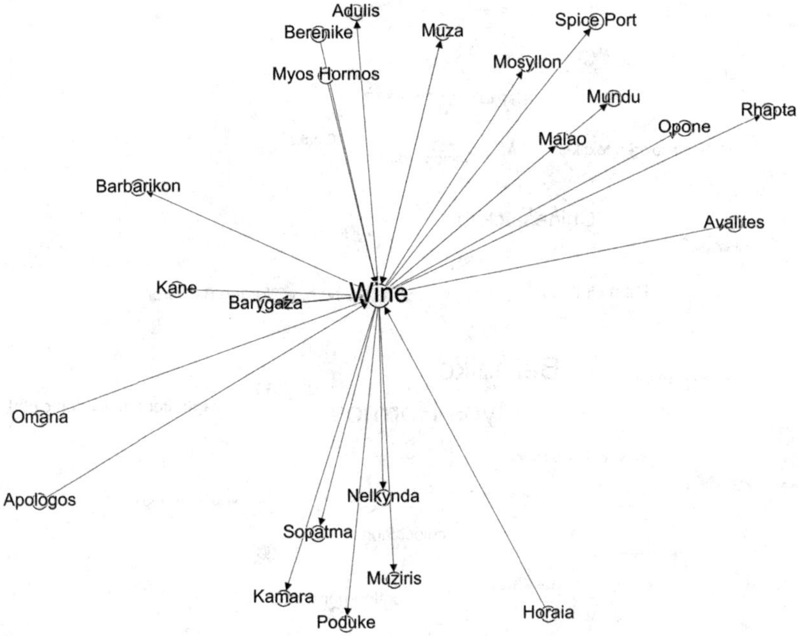

Fig. 4.5 Network of ports importing and exporting wine in the *Periplus Maris Erythraei*. CC BY 4.0 SA

appears to have traveled directly to the Mediterranean by way of ports in Egypt (Fig. 4.6).

South Asian cotton, however, tells a different story. Cotton was imported into a number of ports not only in Egypt, but also in East Africa and Arabia. The reason for this was probably not that people in Arabia and East Africa were not interested in silk, but that the commodity network is an artifact of social networks of traders and allows us to study them. It seems likely that silk was bought by traders from the Roman Empire in ports in India and then brought straight back to Egypt. Cotton also behaved according to this pattern, but in addition to that it was also brought by South Asian traders to ports in Arabia and East Africa. In this manner the network of things also allows us a glimpse into networks of people.

The examples of pepper, money, wine, silk and cotton show how objects move and can be seen as creating their own networks through

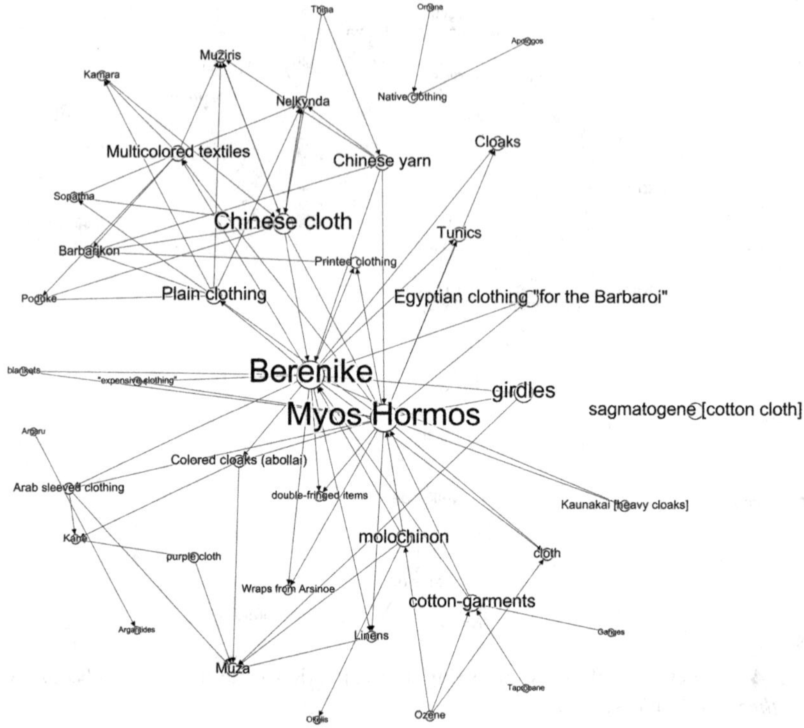

Fig. 4.6 Network of ports importing and exporting textiles in the *Periplus Maris Erythrai*. CC BY 4.0 SA

exchange. While few objects in the real world have the power of the mythological ring of Andvari described at the outset of the chapter, they do have potential to shape the social world around them, and thus they are in possession of agency. If things have agency, they also take part in social networks. Recalling briefly the introduction of this book, Michael Mann identified four sources of social power, namely ideology, economy, military and politics (Mann, 1986). Mann's theory does not directly account for material agency, but objects nevertheless fuel and facilitate these sources of social power. The examples of wine and coins show how imported commodities found symbolic uses in addition to their practical applications and thus became ideological assets in the power-games of elites from southern Scandinavia through South India and China. Objects also had economic impacts, by creating differences between those who had access to them and those who did not, and by giving those who had access the possibility to use objects to get power through redistribution, gift-exchange and trade. Objects of trade, including animals, had obvious military uses, in the form of trade in weapons, diffusion of technologies and use of things for war, and finally things were important in political networks, again due to their symbolic power, which made leaders stand out through conspicuous consumption and generosity with scarce resources.

References

Adams, C. (2007). *Land transport in Roman Egypt: A study of economics and administration in a Roman province*. Oxford University Press.

Appadurai, A. (1986). *The social life of things: Commodities in cultural perspective*. Cambridge University Press.

Axboe, M. (2004). *Die Goldbrakteaten der Völkerwanderungszeit: Herstellungsprobleme und Chronologie: Vol. Bd. 38*. Walter de Gruyter.

Begley, V., Francis, P. J., Mahadevan, I., Raman, K. V., Sidebotham, S. E., Slane, K. W., & Will, E. L. (1996). The ancient port of Arikamedu. In *Mémoires Archeologiques* 22. École Francaise d'Extrême-Orient.

Begley, V., & Ponting, M. (1999). Indian pottery sherds. In S. E. Sidebotham, & W. Z. Wendrich (Eds.) *Berenike 1997. Report of the 1997 excavations at Berenike and the survey of the Egyptian Eastern Desert, including excavations at Shenshef* (pp. 161–182). Universiteit Leiden.

Blue, L. (2009). Boats, routes and sailing conditions of Indo-Roman trade. In R. Tomber, L. Blue, & S. Abraham (Eds.), *Migration, trade and peoples. Part 1: Indian Ocean commerce and the archaeology of Western India* (pp. 3–13). The British Association for South Asian Studies. The British Academy.

Blue, L., Whitewright, J., & Thomas, R. (2011). 15: Ships and ships' fittings. In L. Blue & D. Peacock (Eds.), *Myos Hormos – Quseir al-Qadim. Roman and Islamic ports on the Red Sea. Volume 2: Finds from the excavations 1999–2003* (pp. 179–209). Archaeopress.

Bursche, A. (2002). Circulation of Roman coinage in Northern Europe in late antiquity. *Histoire & Mesure, 17*, 121–141.

Butcher, K. (2020). Introduction. In K. Butcher (Ed.), *Debasement. Manipulation of coin-standards in pre-modern monetary systems* (pp. 1–29). Oxbow Books.

Butcher, K., & Ponting, M. (2014). *The metallurgy of Roman silver coinage: From the reform of Nero to the reform of Trajan*. University Press.

Cappers, R. T. J. (2006). *Roman foodprints at Berenike: Archaeobotanical evidence of subsistence and trade in the Eastern Desert of Egypt*. University of California Los Angeles.

Casson, L. (1989). *The Periplus Maris Erythraei*. Princeton University Press.

Casson, L. (1995). *Ships and seamanship in the ancient world*. John Hopkins University Press.

Cherian, P. J. (Ed.). (2016). *Pattanam excavations. Full reports 2007–2015*. Kerala Council for Historical Research.

Christiansen, E. (1987). *The Roman coins of Alexandria: Quantitative studies*. Aarhus University Press.

Cobb, M. (2018). Black pepper consumption in the Roman Empire. *Journal of the Economic and Social History of the Orient, 61*(4), 519–559.

Cooper, J. P. (2008). *The medieval Nile: Route, navigation and landscape in Islamic Egypt*. University of Southampton.

Crowther, A., Lucas, L., Helm, R., Horton, M., Shipton, C., Wright, H. T., Walshaw, S., Pawlowicz, M., Radimilahy, C., Douka, K., Picornell-Gelabert, L., Fuller, D. Q., & Boivin, N. L. (2016). Ancient crops provide first archaeological signature of the westward Austronesian expansion. *Proceedings of the National Academy of Sciences, 113*(24), 6635–6640.

Cruttenden, C. J. (1849). Memoir on the western or Edoor tribes, inhabiting the Somali coast of N.-E. Africa, with the southern branches of the family of Darrood, resident on the banks of the Webbe Shebeyli, commonly called the River Webbe. *The Journal of the Royal Geographical Society of London, 19*, 49–76.

de la Vaissière, É. (2005). Sogdian Traders: A History. Brill.

De Ligt, L. (1993). *Fairs and markets in the Roman Empire: Economic and social aspects of periodic trade in a pre-industrial society*. Brill.

De Romanis, F. (2012). Playing Sudoku on the verso of the 'Muziris Papyrus': Pepper, malabathron and tortoise shell in the cargo of the Hermapollon. *Journal of Ancient Indian History, 27*, 75–101.

Hall, K. (1999). Coinage, trade and economy in early South India and its Southeast Asian neighbours. *Indian Economic and Social History Review, 36*(4), 432–459.

Hammer, A. (2018). Der Ring der Nibelungen: Der Ring als Ding und Akteur in den skandinavischen und deutschen Versionen des , Nibelungenstoffes'. In A. Bauer & A. Pesch (Eds.), *Hvanndalir – Beiträge zur europäischen Altertumskunde und mediävistischen Literaturwissenschaft* (pp. 97–118). De Gruyter.

Harl, K. W. (1996). *Coinage in the Roman economy, 300 BC to AD 700*. John Hopkins University Press.

Hodder, I. (2012). *Entangled: An archaeology of the relationships between humans and things*. Wiley-Blackwell.

Holleran, C. (2012). *Shopping in ancient Rome: The retail trade in the late republic and the principate*. University Press.

Holleran, C. (2016). Labour mobility in the Roman world: A case study of mines in Iberia. In L. De Ligt & E. Tacoma (Eds.), *Migration and mobility in the early Roman Empire* (pp. 95–137). Brill.

Hoppál, K., Bellina, B., & Dussubieux, L. (2023). Southeast Asia and the Mediterranean world at the turn of the first millennium CE: Networks, commodities and cultural reception. *Cambridge Archaeological Journal*, 1–24.

Juliano, A. L., Lerner, J. A., & Alram, M. (2001). *Monks and merchants: Silk Road treasures from Northwest China: Gansu and Ningxia 4th–7th century*. Asia Society.

Latour, B. (2005). *Reassembling the social—An introduction to actor-network-theory*. Oxford University Press.

Li, Q. (2015). Roman coins discovered in China and their research, Eirene. *Studia Graeca et Latina, 51*(1–2), 279–299.

Loane, H. J. (1944). Vespasian's spice market and tribute in kind. *Classical Philology, 39*(1), 10–21.

MacDowall, D. D. (2004). The Indo-Roman metal trade. In A. Jha & D. W. Mac Dowall (Eds.), *Foreign coins found in the Indian sub-continent* (pp. 40–52). Indian Institute of Research in Numismatic Studies.

Majumdar, S. B. (2016). Money Matters: Indigenous and Foreign Coins in the Malabar Coast (Second Century BCE-Second Century CE). In K.S. Mathew (Ed.) Imperial Rome, Indian Ocean Regions and Muziris (pp. 395-424). Routledge.

Malekandasthil, P. (2016). Muziris and the trajectories of maritime trade in the Indian Ocean in the first millennium CE. In K. S. Mathew (Ed.), *Imperial Rome, Indian Ocean regions and Muziris: New perspectives on maritime trade* (pp. 339–368). Routledge.

Malmberg, S. (2015). 'Ships are seen gliding swiftly along the sacred Tiber': The river as an artery of urban movement and development. In I. Östenberg, S. Malmberg, & J. Bjørnebye (Eds.), *The moving city: Processions, passages and promenades in ancient Rome* (pp. 187–201). Bloomsbury Academic.

Mann, M. (1986). *The sources of social power*. Cambridge University Press.

McConnell, J. R., Wilson, A. I., Stohl, A., Arienzo, M. M., Chellman, N. J., Eckhardt, S., Thompson, E. M., Pollard, A. M., & Steffensen, J. P. (2018). Lead pollution recorded in Greenland ice indicates European emissions tracked plagues, wars, and imperial expansion during antiquity. *Proceedings of the National Academy of Sciences, 115*(22), 5726–5731.

Mitchiner, M. (1976). Greeks, Sakas and their contemporaries in central and southern India. In *Indo-Greek and Indo-Scythian coinage* (Vol. 9). Hawkins Publications.

Mitchiner, M. (2004). The interpretation of foreign coins found in southernmost India. In A. Jha & D. W. Mac Dowall (Eds.), *Foreign coins found in the Indian sub-continent* (pp. 15–24). Indian Institute of Research in Numismatic Studies.

Murphy, N. (2020). The Severan reforms of the late second century AD: A case of monetary déjà vu? In K. Butcher (Ed.), *Debasement. Manipulation of coin-standards in pre-modern monetary systems* (pp. 143–164). Oxbow Books.

Purcell, N. (2016). Unnecessary dependences: Illustrating circulation in pre-modern large-scale history. In J. Belich, J. Darwin, M. Frenz, & C. Wickham (Eds.), *The prospect of global history* (pp. 65–79). Oxford University Press.

Rathbone, D. (2000). The "Muziris" papyrus (SB XVIII 13167): Financing Roman trade with India. *Bulletin De La Société Archéologique D'alexandrie, 46*, 39–50.

Rolnick, A. J., Velde, F. R., & Weber, W. E. (1997). The debasement puzzle: An essay on medieval monetary history. *Federal Reserve Bank of Minneapolis Quarterly Review, 21*(4), 8–20.

Scheidel, W. (2010). The monetary systems of the Han and Roman Empires. In W. Scheidel (Ed.), *Rome and China: Comparative perspectives on ancient world empires* (pp. 137–208). Oxford University Press.

Seland, E. H. (2011). The Persian Gulf or the Red Sea? Two axes in ancient Indian Ocean trade, where to go and why. *World Archaeology, 43*(3), 398–409.

Seland, E. H. (2014). Archaeology of trade in the western Indian Ocean, 300 BC–AD 700. *Journal of Archaeological Research, 22*(4), 367–406.

Seland, E. H. (2016a). Here, there and everywhere: A network approach to textile trade in the *Periplus Maris Erythraei*. In K. Dross-Krüpe & M.-L. Nosch (Eds.), *Textiles, trade and theories: From the ancient Near East to the Mediterranean* (pp. 211–220). Ugarit-Verlag.

Seland, E. H. (2016b). *Ships of the desert and ships of the sea: Palmyra in the world trade of the first three centuries CE*. Harrassowitz.

Seland, E. H. (2016c). The *Periplus of the Erythraean Sea*: A network approach. *Asian Review of World History, 4*(2), 191–206.

Shastri, A. M. (2004). Some aspects of Roman coins in India. In A. Jha & D. W. Mac Dowall (Eds.), *Foreign coins found in the Indian sub-continent* (pp. 45–54). Indian Institute of Research in Numismatic Studies.

Sidebotham, S. E. (2008). Archaeological evidence for ships and harbor facilities at Berenike (Red Sea coast), Egypt. *Memoirs of the American Academy in Rome. Supplementary Volumes*, 6, 305–324.

Sidebotham, S. E. (2011). *Berenike and the ancient maritime spice route*. University of California Press.

Sidebotham, S. E. (2014). Religion and burial at the Ptolemaic-Roman Red Sea emporium of Berenike, Egypt. *African Archaeological Review, 31*, 599–635.

Sidebotham, S. E., Ast, R., Kaper, O. E., Bergmann, M., Bhandare, S., Maurer, A., Hartmann, R., Popławski, S., Oleksiak, J. M., Bartos, N., Geerts, R. C. A., Kucharczyk, R., Castro, M., & Stoye, M. (2023). Results of the Winter 2022 excavation season at Berenike (Red Sea coast), Egypt. *Thetis, 27*, 13–28.

Skre, D. (2025). *The northern routes to kingship: A history of Scandinavia AD 180–550*. Routledge.

Smagur, E. (2018). From coin to bulla: A cultural response to the influx of Roman denarii to India. *Numismatic Digest, 42*, 63–78.

Tomber, R. (2007). Rome and Mesopotamia – Importers into India in the first millennium AD. *Antiquity, 81*, 972–988.

Tomber, R. (2016). The Roman pottery from Pattanam. In K. S. Mathew (Ed.), *Imperial Rome, Indian Ocean regions and Muziris: New perspectives on maritime trade* (pp. 381–394). Routledge.

Turner, P. J. (1989). *Roman coins from India* (Vol. 22). Royal Numismatic Society.

Whitewright, J. (2007). Roman rigging material from the Red Sea port of Myos Hormos. *International Journal of Nautical Archaeology, 36*(2), 282–292.

Zvelebil, K. V. (1956). The Yavanas in Old Tamil literature. In F. Tauer, V. Kubickova, & I. Hrbek (Eds.), *Charisteria Orientalia praecipue ad Persiam pertinentia* (pp. 401–409). Ceskoslovenska Akademie Ved.

CHAPTER 5

Animals

Abstract This chapter highlights the importance and agency of animals in ancient long-distance networks, discussing how they took on roles as producers, commodities, travelers and transporters. Starting with the silk-worm it discusses practicalities of silk production and harvesting of wild silk, and how domestic production in ancient China influenced gender roles and wealth distribution. Finished products traveled with nomads and traders across Central Asia and the Indian Ocean and were exchanged as markers of status and wealth across the Afro-Eurasian world. A brief overview of trade in live animals and animal products is followed by a discussion of trade in horses and mules in the Indian Ocean and of the unintended mobility of the black rat, which spread along the ancient Afro-Eurasian trade networks. The chapter ends with a consideration of the complementary role of different transport animals, from donkeys and mules to Bactrian camels and dromedaries.

Keywords Animal studies · Silk production · Transport animals · Multispecies entanglement · Non-human agency · Trade in animals

© The Author(s), under exclusive license to Springer Nature Switzerland AG 2026

E. H. Seland, *Long-Distance Trade in the Ancient World*, Palgrave Studies in Ancient Economies,
https://doi.org/10.1007/978-3-031-90855-2_5

Many of us live in a world where animals, except for some species of pets and urban scavengers, are concealed in the enclosed pastures and production buildings of modern farms, hiding in the decreasing habitats left to them by human encroachment, or known only from movies and images on our phones. In contrast, animals were ubiquitous in the ancient world. They were sources of food, entertainment, companionship, labor, military power and raw materials, as well as cohabitants and competitors within the same physical spaces that were occupied by humans. Thus, it should perhaps go without saying that they were also deeply entangled in the networks of places, people and things that interconnected the ancient world (Gilhus, 2006; Kalof, 2007; Walker, 2014). Nevertheless, although with notable exceptions (Bulliet, 1975; P. Mitchell, 2018), animals have received little attention within the study of ancient long-distance trade, except as an exotic commodity destined for a bloody end in the Roman arena or for a display of the might of the Roman emperors (Parker, 2008; Scullard, 1974; Toynbee, 1973). In this chapter, we will take case studies of animals serving as producers, products, passengers and transporters within long-distance exchange networks as points of departure to explore some of the contact points and entanglements between animals and humans.

Producers and Products

A humble animal that became immensely important in ancient world-exchange was the silkworm, *bombyx.* In the Mediterranean silk acquired through long-distance trade with the east was most often known as Seric cloth or simply *serikon* in Antiquity. The commodity also provided the Roman name for China and the Chinese—*Sêres*, rather than the other way round. While the etymology is likely Chinese, and cultivated silk was long only produced in central parts of present-day China in the ancient period (Hildebrandt, 2023; Hyllested, 2017), wild silk was also harvested in other places, including in the Mediterranean, but importantly also in South Asia, and Roman historical sources situate the Sêres in various locations in East, Central and South Asia (Kenoyer, 2017; Raschke, 1978). Silk textiles found in archaeological settings include both cultivated and likely wild varieties (Schmidt-Colinet et al., 2000; Zhao, 2017). Cultivation of silk is a highly specialized activity that is archaeologically attested in China from the third millennium BCE, while there is even earlier evidence of silk textiles, presumably based on wild silk (Hildebrandt, 2023; Zanier,

2020). Historically, production of silk thread took place in domestic or manorial spheres, and the production chain, from eggs to finished textiles, was predominantly female work. Taxes levied in woven raw silk forced all households in suitable areas to take part in the industry and made the government a major actor in the processing and redistribution of textiles (Bray, 1997, pp. 191–193, 248–250; Hinsch, 2003) (Fig. 5.1).

The domestic silkworm, ***bombyx mori,*** feeds exclusively on leaves of the white mulberry (***morus alba***) tree, which due to limited durability were mostly cultivated and harvested by silk farmers themselves (Field, 2014, p. 37). Over the course of its five to six weeks' larva-stage, the silkworm grows to a length of up to nine centimeters thereby increasing its size by a factor of 10,000. Over their long existence as a domesticated species, they have lost their ability to survive in the wild, and the larvae need constant feeding, tending and cleaning. When mature, the worm stops eating and starts secreting a continuous silk thread in order to build the cocoon that will protect it during its transformation into a moth (Field, 2014, pp. 26–27). If left to itself, the mature moth will emit enzymes that dissolve part of the cocoon after c. 10 days, enabling it to break out. As this ruins the silk thread, almost all pupae are killed, traditionally by boiling or with a long needle. The few who are spared hatch, mate and lay up to

Fig. 5.1 Silkworms feeding on mulberry leaves, Małgorzata Miłaszewska, CC BY-SA 3.0

500 eggs during the final three to four days of their life. As the domesticated moths, unlike their wild relatives, are unable to fly, this also happens indoor in purpose-built spaces. The eggs mature for about 10 days before hatching, thus restarting the cycle. The intact cocoons of the killed pupae, however, may be unreeled to continuous threads of raw silk that can reach a length of up to 1500 yards (1370 meters). This was woven into rolls of silk that served as important means of tax payment as well as commercial commodities in ancient China (Bray, 1997, pp. 191–193; Field, 2014, pp. 27–29). The domesticated and highly specialized *bombyx mori* is, however, only one out of several species of *bombycidae* that spin fibers that are suitable for textile production. Harvest and production of such so-called wild silk predates the domestic production of silk and has continued alongside it until modern days (Kenoyer, 2017). Most wild silks are coarser than domestic produce and come with degrees of natural coloring or discoloring from the environment, in contrast to the uniform whiteness of domestic silk. Because the thread is chemically and physically damaged when the moth breaks out of the cocoon, wild silk cannot be unreeled as a single thread but needs to be carded and spun. This makes it possible for archaeologists to discern wild and domestic varieties found in archaeological settings, and both are in evidence from sites in Syria (Palmyra) and Central Asia in the early centuries CE (Hildebrandt, 2023; Kenoyer, 2017; Schmidt-Colinet et al., 2000; Zhao, 2017).

As the domestic silkworm feeds exclusively on fresh mulberry leaves and the tending of the insects require intensive work and considerable expertise, the technology of domestic silk rearing for a long time remained restricted to central China. Mulberry trees need to grow for six to eight years before they can be harvested safely and reach maturity only after about twenty years. In arid and semi-arid regions west of China this required investment in and maintenance of stable irrigation systems. Literary and documentary sources show that silk cultivation had reached Khotan in the western Tarim Basin by the second or third century CE, and Merv in Turkmenistan by the seventh century (Zanier, 2020), traveling by the routes outlined in Chapter 2, in this particular case certainly worthy of their Silk Road epithet.

Silkworms live also in the Mediterranean, and Aristotle (*HA*.5.19.6) has a passage, later elaborated on by Pliny the elder (*HN* 1176–77), about the production of wild silk, called by Pliny *bombyx*, on the island of Cos. The report has been met with skepticism among modern scholars, who seek the origin of wild silk found in Mediterranean literature and archaeological settings further east and south (Hildebrandt, 2017). During the first century CE, at the time of the *Periplus of the Erythraean Sea*, Seric silk was available to visiting merchants in South Asian ports in the forms of floss, yarn and cloth (*Periplus* sec. 64; Seland, 2016b). The silk is said to have been produced in the city of Thina, situated adjacent to the Caspian Sea and the sea of Azov, and brought on foot through Bactria to India (*Periplus* sec. 64). Allowing for the lack of first-hand knowledge by the author of the *Periplus* and the poor state of knowledge of areas north and east of the Persianate world in the Roman Empire (Ferguson, 1978; Seland, 2010), this is compatible with a Chinese provenance of first-century silk imported to the Mediterranean. This of course does not rule out that wild silks were also imported from the Indian subcontinent or other sources (Kenoyer, 2017; Raschke, 1978).

During the first to third centuries CE, the Syrian city of Palmyra came to play an important role in the trade between East Asia, Indian Ocean and Mediterranean (Seland, 2016b). No textual sources connect the city with the silk trade, but textiles found in the funerary complexes surrounding the city, where the dead had been mummified and wrapped in strands of cloth, show that silk were among the goods that passed through the oasis. Silks include wild and domestic varieties, while some were undoubtedly processed in China, others are made of thread spun in western tradition or seem to have been embroidered in Asia west of China (Hildebrandt, 2023, p. 502; Schmidt-Colinet et al., 2000), contributing to the impression that Chinese silk was marketed in many forms. After the Roman sack of Palmyra, 272–273 CE, a series of Roman-Sasanian treaties stipulate designated markets in which trade between the empires should take place (Seland, 2016a). At the time of Ammianus Marcellinus (second half of the fourth century CE) this took place in Batnae (present-day Suruç, Türkiye), where an annual fair was held in September (*Res Gestae* 14.3.3). While an edict issued by Honorius and Theodosius, 408 or 409 CE stipulates that Nisibis (Nusaybin), Callinicum (Raqqa) and Artaxata were the only legal places of transaction.

A famous passage from the Byzantine historian Procopius (*Wars* 8.8.7–9) relates how two Indian monks traveled to China or Central Asia (Serinda) on behalf of emperor Justinian in order to smuggle back eggs of the silkworm. The eggs were kept warm in dung and hatched after reaching Constantinople, where the worms were fed with mulberry leaves. A similar account, differing only in the detail that the traveler was a single Persian rather than two Indians, is preserved in Photius' summary of

Theophanes lost *Histories* (*Bibl.* 64, lines 34–73). This has generally been taken as the start of Byzantine sericulture, which over time would become a flourishing trade (Wu, 2023). There is nothing implausible in the story, but it also seems to support that silk remained primarily a commodity of long-distance exchange throughout the pre-Islamic period, as the establishment of domestic production in the Byzantine empire would take time.

The gluttonous, spinning caterpillars from central China were deeply entangled in networks of trade, wealth, diplomacy and power across the ancient world. In the best case they brought wealth, in other cases merely relief from tax claims or corvée burdens to the people who tended the silkworms and wove their threads into bolts of raw silk. In both cases they contributed to the status and economic position of women in Chinese households, who were generally in charge of tending the silkworms as well as of textile production (Bray, 1997, pp. 248–250). The domestically produced textiles were sold or handed over as taxes payment to be rewoven into sumptuous brocades by skilled workers in specialized private and government workshops, or they were forwarded eastwards and northwards as trade goods and subsidies to the nomads living along the imperial Chinese frontiers (Good, 2002). Nomads engaging in redistributive exchange as well as professional traders carried the silk across Central Asia to the Kushan and Arsacid-Sasanid empires, from where it made its way into the Indian Ocean networks and to the Mesopotamian cities where it was offered to Roman merchants. Silk textiles became increasingly common in the Roman empire from the first century onwards, to the delight of Roman consumers and the dismay of the moralists who authored most literary sources of the period. Textiles were woven, patterned and dyed according to Roman taste. In a world clad in wool and linen, expensive and conspicuous imported silk textiles were a certain way of standing out, and soon became a coveted luxury as well as the target of sumptuary legislation (Hildebrandt, 2012). This shows how commodities in ancient world trade took up novel meanings in the lives of the people who consumed them or refrained from using them, even if they knew little or nothing about the long chain of processes that had brought them across the ancient world.

In a world without synthetic processes, the diversity of animals adapted to different ecosystems and climate zones made them attractive sources of trade goods. Silk, with the producing animal becoming dependent on human assistance for its existence and reproduction is arguably among the most outspoken example of animal-human entanglement in ancient world trade, but other animals would fill partly similar roles. Lac, used in glossy varnishes of wood and other surfaces, is made from a secrete from the lac bug (*kerria lacca*), native to South and Southeast Asia. In the first century CE lac from western India was available in the port of Adulis in the southern Red Sea (*Periplus* sec. 6) Pearls were harvested from oysters by divers working under hazardous conditions in shallow waters of the Red Sea, Persian/Arabian Gulf and along the coast of South India and Sri Lanka. Increased demand for luxuries in the Mediterranean in the first century CE seems to have prompted direct response in the form of expanding pearl-fishing activities in the Indian Ocean, and pearls became important in royal and Christological symbology in Late Antiquity (Hope, 2019, 2024; Schörle, 2015).

Related to the role of animals as producers is that of animals that were harvested, hunted or bred in order to sell the animals themselves, parts of them or products derived from them. The purple produced from the murex snail in the eastern Mediterranean thus became one of the most expensive and prestigious commodities in the ancient world, all the more so when used to dye equally expensive Chinese silk (Hildebrandt, 2017). Other coveted pigments used in textile production were harvested from insects (Schmidt-Colinet et al., 2000). So-called Seric pelts, according to the *Periplus* available as a transit commodity in Northwestern India, were likely not from China, but rather furs from Central Asian sable and other animals that arrived on the Indian Ocean rim by way of the same routes as Chinese silk (*Periplus* sec. 39; Liu, 2010, p. 38). Sea tortoise was hunted in many locations in the Indian Ocean region. The shells were cut and polished for use as inlays in furniture, for jewellery, in combs and other small, decorative items (Pliny *NH* 16.232; *Periplus* sec. 30).

Commodities and Passengers

The capture and transport of African and Asian animals as diplomatic gifts for Mediterranean rulers, for display and slaughter in Roman arenas, and of elephants as steeds of war for Hellenistic monarchs have received considerable attention in past scholarship (Kalof, 2007; Parker, 2008; Shelton, 2014; Toynbee, 1973), and it has even been suggested that the North African elephant was hunted to extinction to satisfy Mediterranean demand for beasts of war and entertainment (Casson, 1993; Scullard, 1974). In addition to elephants and large cats, animals captured and shipped as exotica in this manner included monkeys, rhinoceros, peacocks, ostriches, zebras and camels (Toynbee, 1973). The transport, sustenance, and care of many of these large, often tropical animals, proved difficult. They frequently died in captivity before having fulfilled their purpose, and sometimes, as attested by passages in classical literature, failed to perform as hoped if they did (Kalof, 2007, pp. 20–34; Shelton, 2014). Some animals, however, came to stay. The peacock, originally from South Asia, is first attested in the Mediterranean at the time of Ptolemy II (r. 284–246), and must presumably have arrived in Egypt as a trading commodity or a diplomatic gift, but was bred in large numbers in Italy by the late republican period (Toynbee, 1973, pp. 250–251). The chicken (*galli*, several species), hails from Southeast Asia, and is first attested as a domestic animal in present-day Thailand and in China at the turn of the first millennium BCE (Best et al., 2022). Presumably, it must have been domesticated some time before, as it turns up in funerary settings in Italy stemming from the ninth century BCE (Trentacoste, 2020), having arrived in the Mediterranean via maritime networks in the Indian Ocean during a period where few other indications of trans-oceanic connections exist (cf. Seland, 2017a). At first likely to have been exchanged mainly as exotica, the birds seem to spread across the Mediterranean with Greek and Phoenician networks during the first millennium BCE and to mainland Europe with the Romans in the first century CE, gradually turning into an important source of meat and eggs in new regions as the bird became plentiful (Best et al., 2022).

A prominent example of live animals traded in ancient long-distance networks was horses. Horses were used and bred all over the ancient world, apart from Sub-Saharan Africa, where the microbiological environment was particularly hostile to them (P. J. Mitchell, 2018), but throughout the premodern period the best breeding grounds remained areas with large open grasslands, in particular the Eurasian Steppe, extending from Eastern Europe, the northwest Asia and Central Asia (Gommans, 1994), as well as the Iberian peninsula and North Africa (Toynbee, 1973, p. 168). From these areas came the largest and strongest breeds, best suited for purposes of prestige and war and thus for the high-value, high-risk activity of long-distance trade (Clarence-Smith, 2020). Horses, along with peaceful relations, were the main returns offered by the northern neighbors of the Han empire in return for the silk that entered the Eurasian networks across the Chinese borders, and the desire for Central Asian steeds of war seems to have been an important motivation for official Chinese interest in the so-called western regions (Tao, 2019).

Horses were also attractive in South Arabia and South India, where lack of extensive grasslands made breeding difficult. The *Periplus* lists horses and mules among the diplomatic gifts given to South Arabian kings by visiting merchants from the Roman empire (*Periplus* sec. 24). The Tamil epic poem *Pattinappalai*, describing the main port of the Early Historical South Indian Chola kingdom, at the mouth of the Kaveri River, mentions horses as an import arriving by sea (Chelliah, 1962, l. 212). Transporting horses by ship was risky. Journeys were long, ships were cramped, and although military ships designed for the transport of horses are known from the Mediterranean, Indian Ocean ships were not suited to transport large animals safely and in comfort. Modern scholarship on horse trade in the Indian Ocean has pointed to the prosaic, but significant fact, that equids are physically unable to vomit. This would expose them to risk of choking if they became seasick. Moreover, unlike in major Mediterranean ports, there were no deep-water quays in the Indian Ocean. Horses could not be disembarked with cranes, as would be the safest solution, or with gangways, but would have to be ferried ashore in small boats or swim themselves. Animals being weakened by the journey and terrified by the circumstances, risks of drowning or an accident resulting in a broken leg were significant (Clarence-Smith, 2020).

Other animals traveled with humans along the trade networks of ancient Afro-Eurasia without their consent. The black rat, *rattus rattus,* was indigenous to northwest India (Baig et al., 2019). It is not attested in the Mediterranean before the Roman period, and likely reached Egypt first as a passenger of trading ships in the Indian Ocean (McCormick, 2003). McCormick has demonstrated that the earliest finds from the Roman empire are close to the coast and suggests that the animals spread to ports in the Eastern Mediterranean with the grain fleets from Alexandria. Rats thrive on cereals and in close proximity of humans, and over time they spread across the urban network of the Roman world (McCormick, 2003). This, in turn, would facilitate the rapid spread of the *yersina pestis* microbe, which uses rats as one of its preferred vectors, when the first plague pandemic struck across the ancient world in the mid-sixth century (Green, 2020; Harper, 2017; McCormick, 2003).

Transport

One of the prime uses of animals by humans in the premodern world was for transport. Ancient mariners lacked maps. Along with stars, clouds, currents and the color of the water, they used their knowledge of fish and birds to find their way across the ocean, in particular in order to know when they approached low coasts (Arnaud, 2005). In the Indian Ocean, the *Periplus* reports that mariners knew when they finally were approaching the low and dangerous coasts of present-day Gujarat from the presence of sea snakes coming out to meet the ships, a phenomenon also well known to early modern travelers (*Periplus* sec. 40; Seland, 2012).

In a world lacking motorized transport, the prime use of animals, however, was as a source of energy. While horses were used mainly for riding, and were a privilege of the rich in most agricultural societies due to their price and maintenance cost, donkeys had been trotting along the overland routes through Africa, Asia and Mediterranean Europe since the Bronze Age. Donkeys stem from the African wild ass, and the process of domestication seems to have started sometime between 5500 and 4500 BCE (P. Mitchell, 2018, pp. 36–39). Donkeys are excellently adapted to the semi-arid and frequently hot conditions of North Africa, the Middle East and Central Asia. They can subside on protein-low fodder, need a smaller energy to weight ratio compared to horses, and may go without water for up to three days if necessary (P. Mitchell, 2018, pp. 24, 33–39). Donkeys carry up to 90 kilograms of goods over distances of 24–30 kilometers per day (ibid., p. 131). This means they would manage to carry for instance two medium sized amphorae, the standard shipping containers of the Roman world, filled with wine or oil. Donkeys are better suited to rocky and steep terrains than camels and horses. Far from the stupid and stubborn creatures they are often depicted as, they are reliable and persistent animals. It is no coincidence that, unlike other erstwhile pack animals, donkeys continue to have economic importance in many parts of the world even today (P. Mitchell, 2018, pp. 1–4). The overland networks conveying metals and textiles from Central Asia, by way of Mesopotamia and Anatolia to the Levant and Egypt in the Middle Bronze Age, sometimes characterized as the first globalized world system (Frank & Gills, 1993), relied completely on donkey transport and would never have been possible without it (P. Mitchell, 2018, pp. 79–86). Donkeys continued to be important in the classical period, for instance in supplying the Egyptian

Red Sea ports of Berenike and Myos Hormos and the many road stations and mining outposts between them and the Nile, all of which depended on provisions from the Nile Valley (ibid, pp. 138).

Mules, the mostly sterile offspring of a male donkey and a female horse, combine the work capacity and modesty of its father with the size and strength close to that of its mother. Mules became the pack animal of choice in the Roman world, used extensively for commercial transport as well as for the army (Toynbee, 1973, pp. 185–192), and the mules imported into South Arabia according to the *Periplus*, must have been attractive beasts of burden in the mountainous and rocky southern and western parts of the peninsula. But only one kind of animal was able to efficiently cross the immense deserts and dry-steppes that span the Afro-Eurasian landmass while at the same time carrying heavy burdens and living of the land. From its domestication and until the development of fast and efficient sailing ships, and motorized land transport, the camel remained the mainstay of overland communication in arid parts of the world (Bulliet, 1975; Steensgaard, 1974).

There are two species of camel, *camelus dromedarius* and *camelus bactrianus*, known as the dromedary and the Bactrian camel. The one humped, short haired, dromedary thrives in flat, arid and warm climate in Africa, the Middle East and parts of Central and South Asia north of 13 degrees latitude, while the two-humped, ragged, Bactrian camel handles rocky terrain and cold better, and is found at altitudes up to 4000 meters and northwards approximately to 52 degrees latitude, but cannot sustain the consistent warm climate of South Asia, Arabia and North Africa (Gauthier-Pilters & Dagg, 1981, pp. 1, 6; Potts, 2004). Camels are almost exclusively domestic animals. No wild dromedaries have existed in historical times, and only very small, now severely endangered populations of wild Bactrian camels are known (Gauthier-Pilters & Dagg, 1981, pp. 5, 130; Kaczensky et al., 2014).

The Bactrian camel, despite its name, did not origin in the historical landscapes of Bactria, in present-day Afghanistan, but in arid regions of Inner Asia, where the earliest evidence of domestication is c. 5000 years old, opening opportunities for the development of nomadic modes of subsistence in the region (Ji et al., 2009; Potts, 2004). Reviewing the archaeological record, Potts suggest a gradual westward diffusion with Bactrian camels reaching present-day Turkmenistan and Iran over the course of the second millennium CE, and gradually spreading across Iran and into Anatolia during the first half of the first millennium CE. Here it met with the habitats more suitable for the dromedary. The chronology of the domestication of the dromedary has been controversial because the animal figures in the Biblical book of *Genesis*, but reviews of archaeological and textual evidence suggest a date around the turn of the first millennium BCE for the domestication, with the accompanying nomadic lifestyle spreading rapidly throughout the arid West Asia in the following centuries (Magee, 2015; Retsö, 1991; Rosen & Saidel, 2010).

Both Bactrian camels and dromedaries are excellent pack animals. Figures in veterinary- and travel-literature as well as in military handbooks vary considerably, but it is clear that both animals can comfortably cover 30–40 kilometers in a day. In cool conditions they get most of their moisture from the fodder, and even when worked hard and in warm weather, they may go for several days without water. Given adequate care, Bactrian camels may carry c. 250 kilograms and dromedaries approximately 180 kilograms over the prolonged periods of weeks or months required for long-distance connectivity without detrimental effects (P. Mitchell, 2018, p. 131; Potts, 2004; Seland, 2015). The much higher figures for loads, distances and days without water sometimes cited, usually refer to records, emergencies or exceptional occasions such as messengers or expeditions, not infrequently ending with the death of animals. Iconographic depictions of dromedaries (Fig. 5.2) often show them carrying four amphoras, two on each side, or two large bales of packed merchandise, which might have been textiles, aromatics or other dry goods that needed to be protected from the elements (Seland, 2017b).

As with equids it is also possible to cross breed camels. In parts of west and inner Asia, in the ecotones where the habitats of Bactrian camels and dromedaries overlap, the species are crossbred, creating a hybrid that has the size and strength of the Bactrian variety and the dromedary's ability to

Fig. 5.2 Mokhasos the camel-driver with his animals. Byzantine/Early Islamic mosaic, Deir al-Adas, Syria. Jørgen Christian Meyer. CC BY-SA 4.0

survive consistent hot climate. As shown by Potts (2004), hybrids can be traced to the neo-Assyrian period and have a reputation for being superior pack animals to both species.

The advantages over the donkey in terms of capacity and ability are clear, but the camel also offered other benefits. Camels produced meat, milk, wool, leather and dung (for fuel) that allowed people to live as nomads in regions that had hardly been exploited by humans before. Animal herds were mobile and near self-sustained sources of wealth. Nomads accustomed to cover hundreds of kilometres with their animals over the course of a yearly cycle of movement between pastures, became experts in logistics, mounted warfare and animal handling, that also allowed them to engage in long-distance transport. Whereas donkeys would have to be (and were) maintained year-round for intermittent transport purposes, camel herders could use or rent out camels for commercial transport for parts of the year, to fit with the seasonal rythms of long-distance connectivity imposed by climate and harvest times (Seland, 2015).

Animal-Human Entanglement in Ancient Trade

Thus, the two camel species, domesticated at each end of the Asian continent, made possible a first millennium transport revolution, in the same manner that the donkey had enabled the Bronze Age world system. Without the camel, no overland Silk Road between Syria and China (Potts, 2004) and no caravans with spices and aromatics from South Arabia to the Mediterranean. Without donkeys and mules, no Roman empire. In short, pack animals are the unsung heroes of premodern globalization in the same manner that silkworms worked tirelessly to provide tax, rent and clothes in ancient China and beautiful pieces of clothing that would amaze consumers and anger conservative commentators in ancient Rome. One would perhaps imagine that the important role played by these and other animals that took part in ancient world trade, would have earned them gratitude and esteem, this is hardly reflected in the textual and iconographic records. While donkeys and/or onagers figure in Bronze Age iconography as steeds and draft animals for kings, their status fell rapidly in the Iron Age, as horses took their place as animals of war and mules replaced them as work animals among those who could afford it. The only novel to survive intact from the Roman world, Apuleius' *Metamorphosis*, relates the story of a young man, Lucius, who is turned into a donkey after consuming a magic potion. As the plot progresses, he passes from owner to owner, only to be subject to abuse and cruel treatment from most of them. Among the few Roman mosaics depicting pack animals, mostly as part of rural scenes, some show cruelty toward animals, for instance the mosaic from the late Roman church in Petra of a camel carrying a log (Fig. 5.3). The reluctant animal seems to be in agony while it is pulled by one handler and whipped by another. This is in line with Roman attitudes to wild animals, which were considered dangerous, frightening, and whose subjugation, suffering and death during animal spectacles symbolized the unique position of humans (Shelton, 2014).

On the other hand, ethnographic records on show great admiration and affinity for camels among camel herding nomads (e.g., Dickson, 1949; Musil, 1928), although primarily for animals exceptional for their beauty, speed or strength. The description of the misfortunes of Lucius in *Metamorphosis* does distinguish between different owners ill-treating and spoiling the donkey, both exposing their stupidity through their actions. Many ancient animal owners and handlers surely grew fond of and took good care of their charges in the same manner that modern

Fig. 5.3 Pack-camel, Late Roman mosaic from Petra. Eivind Heldaas Seland CC BY-SA 4.0

owners do. Animals had high economic value, well treated animals had higher economic value and carried status. Modern scholarship recognizes the sophistication of ancient animal husbandry, which in many aspects compares favorably with modern factory farming with regard to animal welfare (Kron, 2014).

References

Arnaud, P. (2005). *Les routes de la navigation antique: Itinéraires en Méditerranée*. Éditions Errance.

Baig, M., Khan, S., Eager, H., Atkulwar, A., & Searle, J. B. (2019). Phylogeography of the black rat *Rattus rattus* in India and the implications for its dispersal history in Eurasia. *Biological Invasions, 21*(2), 417–433.

Best, J., Doherty, S., Armit, I., Boev, Z., Büster, L., Cunliffe, B., Foster, A., Frimet, B., Hamilton-Dyer, S., Higham, T., Lebrasseur, O., Miller, H., Peters, J., Seigle, M., Skelton, C., Symmons, R., Thomas, R., Trentacoste, A., Maltby, M., & Sykes, N. et al. (2022). Redefining the timing and circumstances of the chicken's introduction to Europe and north-west Africa. *Antiquity, 96*(388), 868–882.

Bray, F. (1997). *Technology and gender: Fabrics of power in late imperial China*. University of California Press.

Bulliet, R. W. (1975). *The camel and the wheel*. Harvard University Press.

Casson, L. (1993). Ptolemy II and the hunting of African elephants. *Transactions of the American Philological Association, 123*, 247–260.

Chelliah, J. V. (1962). *Pattupattu: Ten Tamil idylls*. South India Saiva Siddhanta Works Publishing Society.

Clarence-Smith, W. G. (2020). Equids across the Indian Ocean, c. 1800–1918. *Journal for Maritime Research, 22*(1–2), 41–57.

Dickson, H. R. P. (1949). *The Arab of the desert*. George Allen & Unwin Ltd.

Ferguson, J. (1978). China and Rome. In H. Temporini & W. Haase (Eds.), *Aufstieg und Niedergang der Römischen Welt: Vol. II.9.2* (pp. 581–601). Walter de Gruyter.

Field, J. (2014). Silk production: Moths, mulberry and metamorphosis. In E. Hallam & T. Ingold (Eds.), *Making and growing* (pp. 25–44). Taylor & Francis.

Frank, A. G., & Gills, B. K. (1993). *The world system: Five hundred years or five thousand?* Routledge.

Gauthier-Pilters, H., & Dagg, A. I. (1981). *The camel: Its evolution, ecology, behavior, and relationship to man*. The University of Chicago Press.

Gilhus, I. S. (2006). *Animals, gods, and humans: Changing attitudes to animals in Greek, Roman, and early Christian ideas*. Routledge.

Gommans, J. (1994). The horse trade in eighteenth-century South Asia. *Journal of the Economic and Social History of the Orient, 37*(3), 228–250.

Good, I. (2002). The archaeology of early silk. *Textile Society of America Symposium Proceedings, 388*, 1–10.

Green, M. H. (2020). The four black deaths. *The American Historical Review, 125*(5), 1601–1631.

Harper, K. (2017). *The fate of Rome: Climate, disease, and the end of an empire*. Princeton University Press.

Hildebrandt, B. (2012). Der Römer neue Kleider: Zur Einführung von Seide im kaiserzeitlichen Rom. In A. Nuss, D. Engster, & G. A. Lehmann (Eds.), *Von der bronzezeitlichen Geschichte zur modernen Antikenrezeption* (pp. 11–53). Universitätsverlag Göttingen.

Hildebrandt, B. (2017). Silk production and trade in the Roman Empire. In B. Hildebrandt & C. Gillis (Eds.), *Silk: Trade & exchange along the Silk Roads between Rome and China in antiquity* (pp. 71–93). Oxbow Books.

Hildebrandt, B. (2023). Roman silk trade and markets. In *The world of the ancient Silk Road* (pp. 497–510). Routledge.

Hinsch, B. (2003). Textiles and female virtue in early imperial Chinese historical writing. *Nan Nü, 5*(2), 170–202.

Hope, D. (2019). Pearls found in ancient Greek and Roman contexts in the Mediterranean. *Mediterranean Archaeology, 32*, 23–122.

Hope, D. (2024). Pearl. In J. Schiettecatte (Ed.), *Thematic dictionary of ancient Arabia*. Centre National de la Recherche Scientifique (CNRS). https://researchers.mq.edu.au/en/publications/pearl

Hyllested, A. (2017). Word migration on the Silk Road: The etymology of English silk and its congeners. In B. Hildebrandt & C. Gillis (Eds.), *Silk: Trade and exchange along the Silk Roads between Rome and China in antiquity* (pp. 61–70). Oxbow Books.

Ji, R., Cui, P., Ding, F., Geng, J., Gao, H., Zhang, H., Yu, J., Hu, S., & Meng, H. (2009). Monophyletic origin of domestic Bactrian camel (*Camelus bactrianus*) and its evolutionary relationship with the extant wild camel (*Camelus bactrianus ferus*). *Animal Genetics, 40*(4), 377–382.

Kaczensky, P., Adiya, Y., von Wehrden, H., Mijiddorj, B., Walzer, C., Güthlin, D., Enkhbileg, D., & Reading, R. P. (2014). Space and habitat use by wild Bactrian camels in the Transaltai Gobi of southern Mongolia. *Biological Conservation, 169*, 311–318.

Kalof, L. (2007). *Looking at animals in human history*. Reaktion Books.

Kenoyer, J. M. (2017). Textiles and trade in South Asia during the proto-historic and early historic period. In B. Hildebrandt & C. Gillis (Eds.), *Silk: Trade and exchange along the silk roads between Rome and China in antiquity* (pp. 33–60). Oxbow Books.

Kron, G. (2014). Animal husbandry. In L. Campbell (Ed.), *The Oxford handbook of animals in classical thought and life* (pp. 109–135). Oxford University Press.

Liu, X. (2010). *The Silk Road in world history*. University Press.

Magee, P. (2015). When was the dromedary domesticated in the ancient Near East. *Zeitschrift Für Orient-Archäologie, 8*, 252–277.

McCormick, M. (2003). Rats, communications, and plague: Toward an ecological history. *The Journal of Interdisciplinary History, 34*(1), 1–25.

Mitchell, P. (2018). *The donkey in human history: An archaeological perspective*. Oxford University Press.

Mitchell, P. J. (2018). The constraining role of disease on the spread of domestic mammals in sub-Saharan Africa: A review. *Quaternary International, 471*, 95–110.

Musil, A. (1928). *The manners and customs of the Rwala Bedouins*. American Geographical Society.

Parker, G. (2008). *The making of Roman India*. Cambridge University Press.

Potts. (2004). Camel hybridization and the role of Camelus bactrianus in the ancient Near East. *Journal of the Economic and Social History of the Orient, 47*(2), 143–165.

Raschke, M. G. (1978). New studies in Roman commerce with the East. In H. Temporini & W. Haase (Eds.), *Aufstieg und Niedergang der römischen Welt: Vol. II.9.2* (pp. 604–1361). Walter De Gruyter.

Retsö, J. (1991). The domestication of the camel and the establishment of the Frankincense Road from South Arabia. *Orientalia Suecana, 40*, 187–219.

Rosen, S. A., & Saidel, B. A. (2010). The camel and the tent: An exploration of technological change among early pastoralists. *Journal of near Eastern Studies, 69*(1), 63–77.

Schmidt-Colinet, A., Stauffer, A., & Al-Asʿad, K. (2000). *Die Textilien aus Palmyra*. Phillipp von Zabern.

Schörle, K. (2015). Pearls, power, and profit: Mercantile networks and economic considerations of the pearl trade in the Roman Empire. In F. De Romanis & M. Maiuro (Eds.), *Across the ocean: Nine essays on Indo-Mediterranean trade* (pp. 43–54). Brill.

Scullard, H. H. (1974). *The elephant in the Greek and Roman world* (Vol. 288). Thames and Hudson London.

Seland, E. H. (2010). *Ports and power in the Periplus: Complex societies and maritime trade on the Indian Ocean in the first century AD*. Archaeopress.

Seland, E. H. (2012). Death or taxes: Choosing itineraries between the Persian Gulf and the Mediterranean in the mid-18th century. *Academic Quarter, 4*, 97–108.

Seland, E. H. (2015). Camels, camel nomadism. And the practicalities of Palmyrene caravan trade. *ARAM, 27*, 45–53.

Seland, E. H. (2016a). Ancient trading networks and New Institutional Economics: The case of Palmyra. In K. Droß-Krüpe, S. Föllinger, & K. Ruffing (Eds.), *Antike Wirtschaft und ihre kulturelle Prägung* (pp. 223–234). Harrassowitz Verlag.

Seland, E. H. (2016b). Here, there and everywhere: A network approach to textile trade in the Periplus Maris Erythraei. In K. Dross-Krüpe & M.-L. Nosch (Eds.), *Textiles, trade and theories: From the ancient Near East to the Mediterranean* (pp. 211–220). Ugarit-Verlag.

Seland, E. H. (2017a). The archaeological record of Indian Ocean engagements in the Red Sea. In *Oxford handbooks online*. Oxford University Press. http://www.oxfordhandbooks.com/view/10.1093/oxfordhb/9780199935413.001.0001/oxfordhb-9780199935413-e-51

Seland, E. H. (2017b). The iconography of caravan trade in Palmyra and the Roman Near East. In A. H. Sørensen & T. Reeves (Eds.), *Position and profession in Palmyra* (pp. 106–114). Royal Danish Academy of Sciences and Letters.

Shelton, J.-A. (2014). Spectacles of animal abuse. In L. Campbell (Ed.), *The Oxford handbook of animals in classical thought and life* (pp. 461–477). Oxford University Press.

Steensgaard, N. (1974). *The Asian trade revolution of the seventeenth century: The East India companies: And the decline of the caravan trade*. University of Chicago Press.

Tao, J. (2019). Heavenly horses of bactria: The creation of the Silk Road. *Emory Journal of Asian Studies, 1*, 1–24.

Toynbee, J. M. C. (1973). *Animals in Roman life and art*. Cornell University Press.

Trentacoste, A. (2020). Fodder for change: Animals, urbanisation, and socio-economic transformation in protohistoric Italy. *Theoretical Roman Archaeology Journal, 3*(1).

Walker, B. L. (2014). Animals and the intimacy of history. In A. C. Isenberg (Ed.), *The oxford handbook of environmental history* (pp. 52–75). Oxford University Press.

Wu, G. (2023). Reconstructing the Byzantine sericulture practice. *Byzantinische Zeitschrift, 116*(3), 1013–1034.

Zanier, C. (2020). The silk cycle in China and its migration. In G. Riello, D. Schäfer, & L. Molà (Eds.), *Seri-Technics: Historical silk technologies* (pp. 13–31). Max-Planck-Gesellschaft zur Förderung der Wissenschaften.

Zhao, F. (2017). Domestic, wild or unraveled? A study on tabby, taqueté and jin with spun silk from Yingpan, Xinjiang, third–fourth centuries. In B. Hildebrandt & C. Gillis (Eds.), *Silk: Trade and exchange along the Silk Roads Between Rome and China in antiquity* (pp. 152–168). Oxbow Books.

CHAPTER 6

Spaces

Abstract The final chapter introduces the concept of space as different from place. Adapting Edward Soja's concept of lived space to one of historical space, it is argued that this allows us to study the integration in time and place of the social and material networks that have been described in previous chapters. This argument is developed through discussions of seascapes, landscapes and cityscapes. Ancient seascapes are approached through descriptions of visual sailing aids in the Red Sea and Gulf of Aden. A map of the East African kingdom of Axum in the sixth century CE gives insight into the historical landscape of that region, while cityscapes, exemplified with the archaeological remains of the Syrian city Palmyra, open windows to the lived worlds of urban populations almost two millennia ago. The book ends with a brief epilogue drawing together the conclusions from the previous chapters on places, people, things and animals, restating the argument for network theory as a means to integrate the discussion of these phenomena within a unified framework.

Keywords Spatial turn · Historical space · Navigation · Maps · Urban topography · Thirdspace

© The Author(s), under exclusive license to Springer Nature Switzerland AG 2026

E. H. Seland, *Long-Distance Trade in the Ancient World*, Palgrave Studies in Ancient Economies,
https://doi.org/10.1007/978-3-031-90855-2_6

Historical geographers have long been aware that "history takes place," by which they mean that we need to take the physical environment into account when we are approaching the past (Kinda, 2017). In 1597 the Flemish cartographer Abraham Ortelius published his *Parergon* (Fig. 6.1), which means an embellishment or decoration. The *Parergon* was a historical atlas of the ancient world, intended to supplement his world atlas called *Teatrum Orbis Terrarum*, the "Theatre of the spherical earth." Map 36 covered the Indian Ocean and parts of the Mediterranean (Ortelius, 1597). It was based primarily on the first century CE Greek text known as the *Periplus of the Erythraean Sea*, which had been translated into Italian and printed by the Venetian scholar Giovanni Battista Ramusio 47 years earlier (Marcotte, 2017; Ramusio, 1550). It also, however, included information from other ancient texts including the Homeric *Odyssey*, the so-called *Periplus of Hanno*, describing Carthaginian explorations along the coast of West Africa, and even a map of then recent European journeys of discovery in the polar regions, the latter in order to demonstrate that the modern explorers and cartographers were not inferior to their ancient forerunners.

With regard to Ortelius' claim that modern (i.e., late sixteenth century) cartography was superior to anything produced in the Roman period, he was justified. During the first half of the sixteenth-century European cartographers had been able to develop projections that gradually improved that of Ptolemy, whose second century CE *Geography* had been preserved in Byzantine libraries, but which was only rediscovered in Western Europe at the turn of the fourteenth century (Fig. 6.2). In many ways this culminated in Gerardus Mercator's projection, published in 1569, which remains the most popular and arguably most practical way of depicting the spherical earth on a flat surface, even today (Dalché, 2007; Snyder, 2007). The claim about superior knowledge about Asia and Africa in Europe and the Mediterranean is more problematic, as Ptolemy's and Pliny's work, the *Periplus*, and many other text, reveal that extensive knowledge of Asia and Africa did exist among many people in the Roman world, although it somehow only to a limited degree transcended into literary and proto-scientific works (Parker, 2008; Schulz, 2024).

Ortelius, in creating his historical map, was fixing a textual narrative from the distant past in a two-dimensional visual representation of three-dimensional physical space. In doing this he combined and reconciled the geographical knowledge accumulated in the ancient period with that gathered during more than a century of early modern European

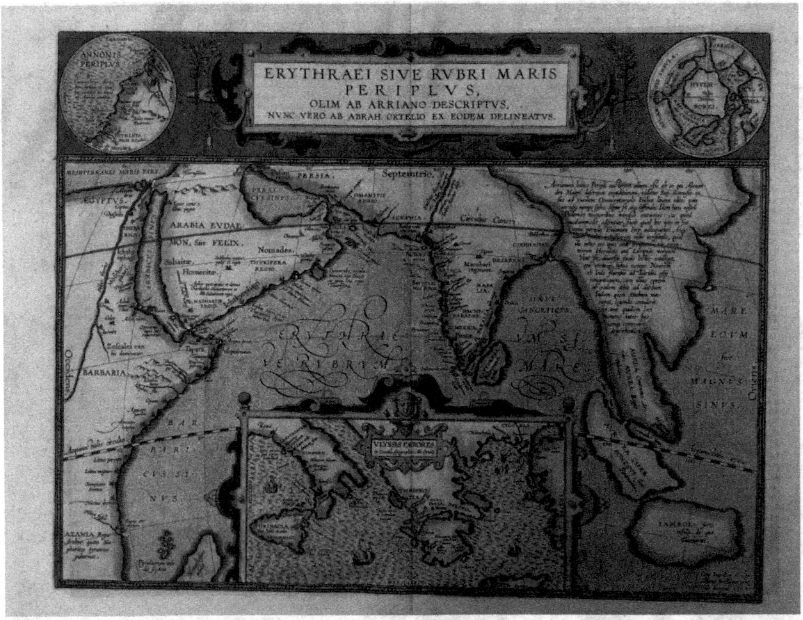

Fig. 6.1 Ortelius map of the ancient Indian Ocean (1597) (*Photo* Eivind Heldaas Seland CC-BY 4.0)

trade, exploration and colonialism in the Indian Ocean. Until a few decades ago, his map could still have served as a decent representation of modern knowledge of ancient trade and navigation in the Indian Ocean, in the sense that this was still largely based on the Roman period literary accounts. This, however, has changed tremendously. New and critical editions and commentaries have been made of the literary sources, but more importantly there has been an explosion in the volume of available archaeological information (cf. Abraham, 2023; Ray, 2003; Seland, 2014, 2017, 2020b; Sidebotham, 2011; Tomber, 2008). This allows us to fix the position of quite a few of the places mentioned in ancient texts and depicted on Ortelius' map, to study their settlement history, and their contact with other places by way of proxies of things that were produced elsewhere, and to identify centers of habitation, production and exchange that were not included in the literary sources. Ceramics have been very important in this, but also botanical material including

Fig. 6.2 Fifteenth-century Ptolemaic world map. New York Public Library, Public Domain

remains of foods, textiles and ships (e.g., Cappers, 2006; Sidebotham, 2011; Tomber, 2008; Wendrich et al., 2003). We also, mostly by way of epigraphy, know much more about the people who were traveling and trading, what script they used, and, in some instances, what place they called home (Fauconnier, 2012; Ray, 2006; Sidebotham, 2011; Strauch, 2012). Lastly, we even know a bit more about the ships that sailed the Indian Ocean from ethnographic studies and from finds made in ports in ancient Egypt (Blue et al., 2011; Sidebotham, 2008; Whitewright, 2007), although not much, as due to preservation the remarkable wreck sites found for instance in Sri Lanka, Saudi Arabia and Eritrea show only remains of the cargo and not of the ship as such (Gaur et al., 2014; Pedersen, 2015). Many of these advances we owe to the so-called spatial turn in the social sciences. Awareness of the importance of place and space in human history in combination with GIS tools and satellite mapping increasingly allow us to understand how historical and archaeological data correlate with the physical environment.

From Place to Space

Critical geographers, however, warn that the triad history, geography, society needs to be fully integrated, because only then we might able to move from geographical place to space, which in difference to place, in that it not only has a physical existence, but also social and temporal (i.e., historical) dimensions, and which appears as a result of interaction between these (Massey, 2005; Soja, 1996). Space does not have an independent existence, but results from such meetings. American geographer Edward Soja, in turn drawing on the work of the French philosopher Henri Lefebvre, operated with three categories of space: Firstspace is perceived space (or spatial practice). Secondspace is conceived space (or representations of space), and thirdspace is lived space (or spaces of representation) (Soja, 1996, pp. 66–82).

Perceived space, or firstspace, is the observable spatial patterns of people, places and things in time, that is the things we can see, count and measure. Archaeologists with the assistance of other scientists, have become increasingly good at this over recent decades, adopting GIS and remote sensing technologies. We might study, for example, how ports are distributed along Mediterranean and Indian Ocean coasts, where the harbor facilities, warehouses and living quarters were situated within these ports, and what groups were active or resident in different neighborhoods of the port at different periods of time based on epigraphy, ceramics, diet or debris from any kind of human activities (e.g., Carannante et al., 2022; Radowska & Zych, 2019; Sidebotham, 2004; Thomas, 2012). Past patterns of behavior that become visible in the archaeological record emerge from a combination of environmental, pragmatic and deliberate decisions. Ports for instance needed water supply, and sheltered anchorage would be a clear advantage. These are to a large extent environmentally determined factors, although within limits they could be provided by human effort. At the Egyptian Red Sea port of Berenike, the location of the settlement was likely determined by the promontory of Ras Banas, offering ships shelter from the prevailing northern winds, and reefs south of the harbor site, sheltering the roadstead from the ocean swell (Hydrographer of the Navy, 1944, pp. 178–180). This meant that water for consumption by animals and humans had to be brought in by pack animals or porters from the closest springs, located c. eight kilometers away (Sidebotham, 2011, pp. 102–103). How settlements were created would, however, to some extent rely on pragmatic factors such as available manpower, expertise and resources. Some spatial decisions, such as where to place the main temple, where the government warehouses and customs posts should be situated, or where the foreign merchants should live, could at least potentially be ascribed to deliberate economic, ideological or political considerations. But once such decisions were made, they laid down patterns that had a tendency to prevail. Many ports in the Indian Ocean were active for centuries, interrupted by periods of decline or abandonment. While this comes close to stating the obvious, it underlines the point that spaces are produced, and that not only geography, but also temporality (i.e., history), and society have a place in that process.

Conceived space (representation of spaces, also secondspace) is our mental models of the world, as we see it, for instance in written and visual representations. The text of the *Periplus*, Ptolemy's *Geography*, the imperial Chinese, Han-period descriptions of the western regions known as the *Ho-Han-Shu* are all examples of this, as are the Byzantine period maps of the Indian Ocean region from Kosmas Indikopleustes *Christian Topography* that will be discussed below. Ortelius map of the ancient Indian Ocean is also a visualization of a conceived space, where the information from Greek and Roman texts serves to justify and glorify early modern European expansion in the Indian Ocean. The same goes for the concepts, descriptions and network graphs used by modern scholars in their attempt to grasp past realities. To complicate this further the only way of recording and sharing perceived spaces is by means of conceived spaces, that is through their representations whether oral, written or visual.

Lived space (spaces of representation, thirdspace) is the most challenging to capture, as it describes how each of us navigate our physical and social surroundings, including symbols, ideologies and power dynamics. This not only varies from person to person, but is also quite hard to form an informed opinion about, because most of our actions and interactions take place without much thought being given to their symbolic implications. Lived space is thus by definition subjective. Different reactions to modern day memorials represent recent examples. Monuments that for some represent heritage and local identity, are perceived as symbols of racism, slavery and oppression by others. In many cases the monuments only become important when they become contended (Legg, 2025). This

Fig. 6.3 The production of historical space (Seland, 2022). CC BY-SA 4.0

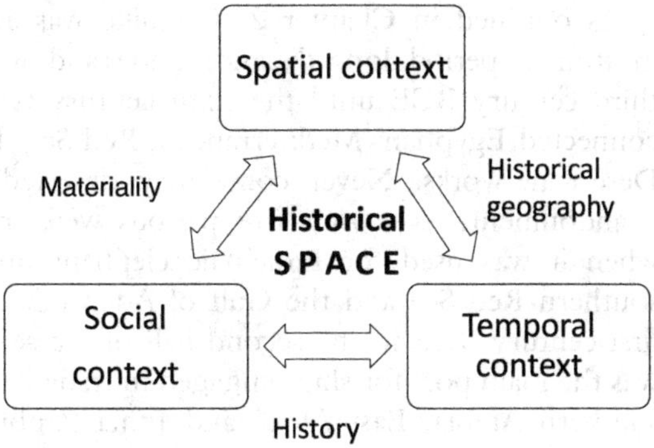

illustrates how history and society come together in actual physical places (Fig. 6.3).

Although we speak of perceived, conceived and lived spaces as separate categories, they depend on each other and overlap (Soja, 1996). We use tools to measure, describe and visualize them, and thus they are all representations of space, that is conceived spaces. Most of these representations are also examples of spatial practice, and thus perceived spaces, and at the moment they become invested with meaning, they also become lived spaces, or spaces of representation (Seland, 2022).

Seascapes

Whereas maps of Asia and the Indian Ocean drawn on basis of Ptolemy's second-century *Geography* (Fig. 6.2) appear unfamiliar to most modern viewers, Ortelius' map is instantly recognizable. Still, lack of knowledge and instrumental measurements cause inaccuracies on the scale of hundreds of kilometers, rendering the map useless beyond its intended purposes of illustration and decoration. Accurate maps of the Indian Ocean littorals were made only in the nineteenth century for navigation purposes and in the twentieth century for land. Detailed maps have in many cases been restricted for military purposes, and high-resolution satellite imagery has only become available and affordable for non-military research purposes and the public over the last two decades. Early travelers in the Mediterranean and Indian Ocean most likely did not have maps at all, they saw the world from the deck of a ship (Arnaud, 2005, pp. 46–49).

As outlined in Chapter 2, Berenike was an important gateway city in Roman period long-distance trade and was in operation from the third century BCE until the sixth century CE (Sidebotham, 2011). It connected Egyptian, Mediterranean, Red Sea, Indian Ocean and Eastern Desert networks. Never completely deserted before its sixth-century abandonment, its most active periods were in the third century BCE, when it was used for Ptolemaic elephant hunting expeditions to the southern Red Sea and the Gulf of Aden (Casson, 1993), from the late first century BCE to the second half of the second century CE, when it was the main port for ships engaged in trade between the Roman empire, southern Arabia, East Africa and India (Cobb, 2015), and the fourth century CE, when it was a main point of contact between the Roman empire and its trading partners in the southern Red Sea (Sidebotham, 2002).

As mentioned, Berenike held a sheltered location on the south side of the peninsula of Ras Banas. Water was available, even if at some distance, and it connected to the extensive route network of the Eastern Desert. Additional advantages were a suitable anchorage at the neck of the peninsula, an approach relatively free of the reefs that line much of the Red Sea coast (Hydrographer of the Navy, 1944, pp. 176–177), and a location sufficiently far south to allow sailors approaching from the Arabian sea to utilize southerly winds prevailing in the early months of the year (Facey, 2004).

Ships leaving from Berenike could use the conspicuous peaks of the coastal mountains to the west, the spit of Ras Banas to the east, and the small island of Mukawwa, some seven kilometers offshore, to find their direction. In fair weather this would keep sailors in sight of land until they saw the island of Zeberget/St. John. Leaving Zeberget behind, mariners would be in the deep, middle channel of the Red Sea, safe from reefs and able to proceed southwards even at night or under conditions of reduced visibility (Hydrographer of the Navy, 1944, pp. 176–180; Seland, 2020a). In this way, we may move from the perceived space of measurements to the conceived space of representations, in this case in modern maps and navigational aids, to put ourselves in the lived space of the people who were navigating the Red Sea two millennia ago (Figs. 6.4–6.5).

In the eastern Mediterranean, the use of topographical features invested with divine identifications as navigational aids is traceable to Late Bronze Age and Phoenician texts, and well attested in the Hellenistic and Roman periods (Collar, 2017). Agatharchides' *On the Red Sea*, a

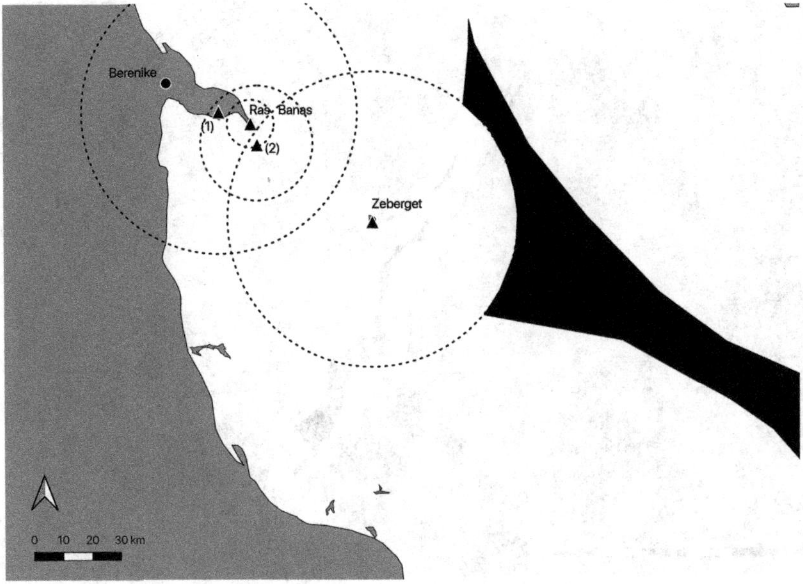

Fig. 6.4 Navigational aids and visibility at the port of Berenike (Seland, 2020a) CC BY-SA 4.0

text from the second century BCE known only from fragments in later texts, reveals the use of mountains as navigational aids in the Red Sea in the Hellenistic era. Navigational poems survive from the Islamic period. These served as mnemotechnic devices, and were to be recited a given number of times, before the relevant sailing mark should appear in sight and the navigator would know what do next, provided that he was reciting at the right pace and that the ship was sailing at the right speed that is (Aḥmad ibn Majīd & Tibbetts, 1971). Until the modern period sailors have marked out and named landmarks that would help them identify their position. Echoes of such may be found in maritime itineraries, geographical descriptions and also toponyms. In the Indian Ocean two of the more conspicuous are situated on opposite sides of the Gulf of Aden. Ras Fartak, Greek *Akroterion Syagros*, is an almost 900 meters tall headland at the head of the Dhofar Bay of present-day Oman. The name means "Cape Boar," both in Arab and in Greek. The name of the mountain is explained by the shape of its relief when seen from the southwest

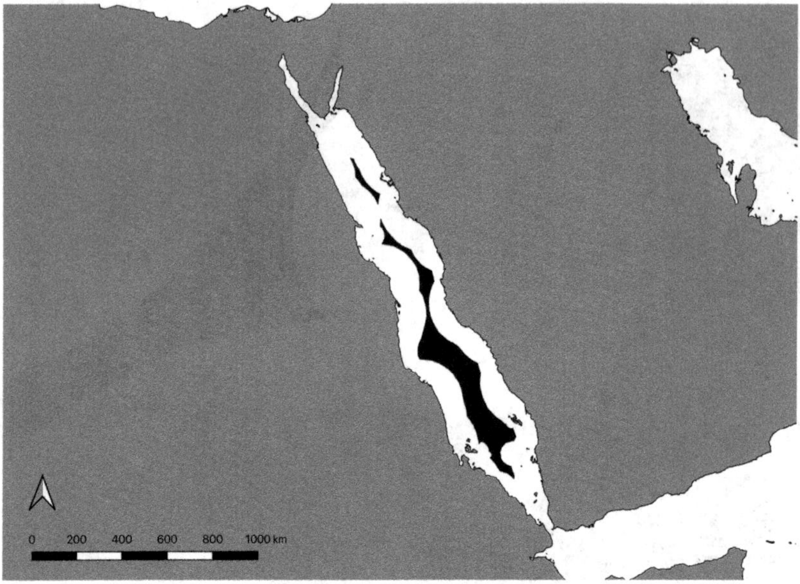

Fig. 6.5 Sea to land visibility in the Red Sea (Seland, 2020a) CC BY-SA 4.0

or from the east (Hydrographer of the Navy, 1944, p. 402), that is when sailing along the Arabian coast. At Ras Filuk/Akroterion Elephas/Capo Elefante on the Somali coast of the Gulf, the west-facing profile of the 246 meters tall headland leaves little to the imagination. It is significant that these names carry the same meaning in Arabic as in Greek, and in the latter case also in Portuguese, highlighting continuity and knowledge transfer over discovery in different premodern traditions of Indian Ocean navigation. This is an example of how the conceived space of maps and place-names, can be fixed as perceived space in GIS software, and allow us to glimpse the lived space of the people who navigated the Gulf of Aden two millennia ago.

In Mediterranean historiography there has been a longstanding debate about whether and to what extent ancient mariners would sail beyond waters with visibility of the coast (Arnaud, 2005, pp. 29–33; Brugge, 2017; Rougé, 1981, pp. 21–23). One group of scholars, many of them belonging to the minimalist camp in the debate on the nature of the ancient economy (cf. Chapter 1), emphasized how visibility of land

(Fig. 6.6) removed the necessity of crossing the open sea, and how lack of instruments made high-sea navigation difficult and dangerous, especially during the winter (Finley, 1973, p. 130; Horden & Purcell, 2000, p. 126; Lane, 1963). Others have pointed to the considerable literary evidence of ancient navigation during night and across the open sea, and that the coast with its cliffs, rocks and shallows represents a more imminent danger to a ship than open waters (Arnaud, 2005, pp. 29–33; Beresford, 2013, pp. 171–177, 183–185, 199–209; Casson, 1995, pp. 270–300; Rougé, 1981, pp. 21–23; Warnking, 2015, pp. 134–135, 176–178). Both points of view find support in that it seems clear that some seafaring cultures in some periods of Mediterranean history and in some parts of the Mediterranean Sea did prefer to stay close to the coast and put in at night. Others, especially those crossing the eastern and southern parts of the Mediterranean, could not avoid crossing large tracts of water beyond theoretical visibility of the coast, and would be well advised to stay clear of the shallow waters with heavy swells and lack of sheltered anchorage along the North African coast east of Carthage (present-day Tunisia) (Seland, 2020a). It has been argued that over time, weather patterns and hydrographic conditions in combination with experience and habit, created customary high-sea lanes that worked similar to highways on dry land (Arnaud, 2005; Warnking, 2015). Similar practices are in evidence in the Red Sea and western Indian Ocean. The coasts of the Red Sea are littered with sharp rocks and reefs. These posed a hazard for shipping, but also, unlike in the Mediterranean, made it possible to anchor small ships overnight in offshore locations (Seland, 2009, 2020a). The exception, however, were big vessels, that because of their draught and windage would be unable to anchor safely, such as the ships that sailed directly between Egyptian Red Sea ports and ports in the Southern Red Sea, Gulf of Aden and along the West coast of India (*Periplus,* sec. 10, 16, 20, 56, 57).

Landscapes

Returning to the concept of the lived space (spaces of representation), one of the defining traits is that these landscapes are charged with meaning for the people who inhabit them (Soja, 1996). Naming mountains after the animals they resemble, as was the case with Ras Fartak and Capo Elefante/Ras Filuk, are basic examples of this. Even more significant is

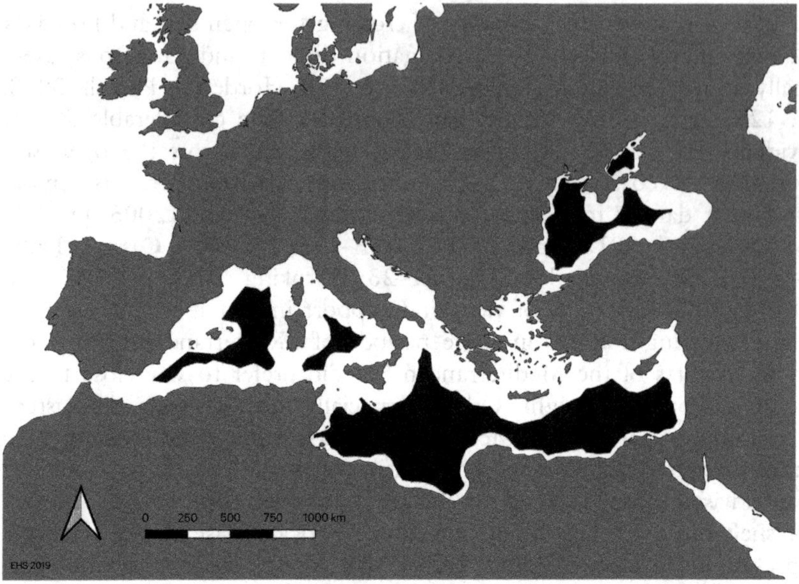

Fig. 6.6 Sea to land visibility in the Mediterranean Sea (Seland, 2020a) CC BY-SA 4.0

the investment of political or religious symbolism into places, as indicated by the identification of landmarks abroad with those familiar from home (Collar, 2017), or the foundation of new settlements on foreign ground with names from the old country. The latter phenomenon was widespread during the early Hellenistic period, when Greek-Macedonian settlers imposed their control on regions in the Red Sea, North Africa and the West Asia. Thus Classical geographical literature contains a confusing array especially of Macedonian dynastic names, but also of transposed Egyptian and Greek toponyms in the southern Red Sea (Cohen, 2006, pp. 307–343). How this tradition left traces that prevailed throughout the Long Classical Millennium is illustrated in a small map that accompanies manuscripts of a sixth century text known as the *Christian Topography* (Fig. 6.7). The text is ascribed to a certain Kosmas Indikopleustes (literally "who sailed to India"), but the actual name of the author is not known for certain. The map is a representation of the Aksumite kingdom in present-day Ethiopia and Eritrea, which Kosmas visited as a merchant,

c. 520 CE. It is not known whether the map was originally drawn by Kosmas himself or if it has been added by the monks who copied the manuscripts at a later stage (Kominko, 2013), but one argument for it being part of the original work is that it contains information which is not found in the accompanying text.

Kosmas' map is itself an example of conceived space, but one which gives a representation of lived space in the sense that it is a visualization of how an observer understood the text it accompanied. The map exemplifies how geography, society and history came together during the visit of Kosmas. On the left side we see the Red Sea littoral and three cities. The coast represents the limit between the maritime space of the Red Sea and the sociopolitical space of the Aksumite kingdom, while the settlements serve as gateways between them. Adulis was the main market of the

Fig. 6.7 Kosmas' map of the Aksumite kingdom. After manuscript Vat.gr.699, 15v. Eivind Heldaas Seland. CC BY-SA 4.0

Aksumite kingdom. It is described as a lawful market, *emporion nomimon*, in the *Periplus* (sec. 6–8), mentioned in a number of later classical sources, and archeologically attested and documented through a series of surveys and excavations (Zazzaro et al., 2014; Zazzaro, 2013, 2017). Through these we know that in the sixth century CE, Adulis was a sizable city with several churches and elite residences, but that is was actually situated a small distance from the shore. Gabaza, is described a customs house (*telônion*). In another sixth century CE source, the *Martyrium sancti Arethae* (29) it is described as the harbor of Adulis. There is also an archaeologically and topographically based suggestion for the exact location (Peacock et al., 2004), thus far not confirmed. The third settlement is an otherwise unknown place named Samidi, situated north of Adulis.

In the upper part of the map, four people, labeled in the legend as Ethiopic foot-soldiers (*aithiopes pezeuontes*), are moving along what is described as the road to Axum, which we know from other literary sources to be the capital (*mêtropolis*) of the kingdom. The status of Axum in relation to Adulis is not mentioned by Kosmas or on the map, but is arguably reflected in the iconography, Axum being represented by a three-domed building, whereas the other settlements are depicted with one dome only. At the center of the map are two monuments, on which most of the scholarly interest has focused (Bowersock, 2013; Kirwan, 1972; Speidel, 2016). In the text of the *Christian Topography* (2.58–2.64) they are said to be situated along this road outside Adulis. These are a stela from the third Macedonian king of Egypt, Ptolemy III (ruled 246–222/221 BCE), commemorating his wars in Syria and his elephant-hunts in the Red Sea, and an inscribed marble throne. The inscribed throne was believed by Kosmas to also belong to Ptolemy but has been demonstrated by modern scholars to actually have commemorated the military exploits of an Axumite king of the second or third century CE. The inscriptions have never been found, but are cited by Kosmas, and based on parallels in Egypt as well as in Aksum, there is no good reason to doubt that they were actually there 1500 years ago, and the inscription on the throne, known as the *Monumentum adulitanum*, is generally considered to be an authentic document of Aksumite history (Bowersock, 2013; Speidel, 2016). At the end of his description, Kosmas adds that the site of the throne was used as a place of execution at the time of his visit (*Christian Topography* 2.64).

Even if it is of limited use as a topographic map in our sense, the map does take firstspace or perceived space into account in its placement of the sea and of the different cities. It also reflects a political hierarchy between settlements, in iconography, in labels, and certainly when taking the text that it relates to into account. Moreover, it reflects several temporal and historical layers: Ptolemaic expansion in the third century BCE, Aksumite expansion in the third century CE, and the contemporary setting of the sixth century CE Christian kingdom of Aksum. The past monuments were used to legitimize the present sociopolitical order to the extent that criminals were executed in this symbolic presence of kings both past and present. In this sense, this secondspace or conceived space document, representing firstspace or perceived space as it appeared at different times of Aksumite history, also gives insight into the thirdspace, the lived space or the space of representation of sixth-century Ethiopia and Eritrea (Seland, 2022).

Cityscapes

A second example of a map representing historical space as well as geographical space is found on the late fourth or early fifth century CE Roman route map known as the *Tabula Peutingeriana* (Fig. 6.8.), which, however, also contains layers of earlier information (Rathmann, 2018; Talbert, 2010; Weber, 1976). Panel XII, depicting southern India and Sri Lanka, shows the harbor town of Muziris, probably the archaeological site of Pattanam in Kerala (Cherian, 2016, see also Chapter 4). Muziris on the Peutinger map has a *templ(um) Augusti*—a temple of the divine Roman Emperors.

The map depicts places with their distances between them, although presented in the manner of communication lines rather than the accurate rendering of geographical space and landforms, much in the manner of a modern tube map or network graph. The central segments of the map, displaying the Mediterranean region provide a fairly accurate representation of perceived space, considering the time it was produced in. In the depiction of South India, however, there is very little accuracy left. In part this surely reflects inadequate knowledge of the region. In part it was arguably never intended as an accurate depiction, but rather to underline the greatness of Rome (Talbert, 2010), and this is surely one relevant reading of the Roman temple in South India, namely that the Romans looking at the map would be able to say to themselves that even at the end of the known world there is a temple to our emperors. This would be a similar kind of conceived space to Ortelius' map from the turn of

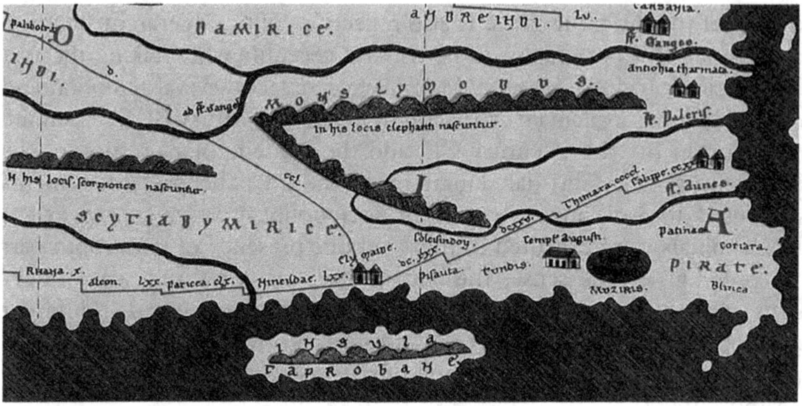

Fig. 6.8 Temple of the Roman emperors in Muziris, South India on the Tabula Peutingeriana. Reproduced from Miller, K. (1887). *Weltkarte des Castorius genannt die Peutinger'sche Tafel*, Maier. Public Domain

the seventeenth century, intended to show that modern exploration and knowledge of Asia was superior to that of ancient times. As a secondspace representation of what was going on in South India in the fourth or fifth century CE, however, the *Tabula* is likely misleading. While the imperial cult continued to be celebrated in a Roman empire that was firmly Christian at the time (Trombley, 2011), Roman direct contacts with South India were to our knowledge relatively limited.

Two to three centuries earlier, however, things had been different. There was an active, regular and apparently, rather large-scale traffic between Egypt and South India. Very likely there was also a settlement of Roman subjects in Muziris, just as there were settlements of South Asia merchants in Berenike and on Socotra (Chapter 2). It seems plausible that Romans would celebrate the imperial cult there, as a way of maintaining cohesion among themselves, in the same manner that residents of South Asian origin seem to have maintained Buddhist cultic practices in ports they visited. These places likely functioned as much as social clubs for Roman expatriates and visitors as they did as foci of religious worship, but this does not imply that their role was unimportant (Metzler, 1989; Seland, 2016b; Chapter 3). In this context the Roman temple in South India does make sense. The sanctuary provided a social space for Roman subjects who were in India, which connected them with those taking part in the imperial cult elsewhere, inside and outside the borders of the Roman Empire.

Historical spaces may also be traced in urban topographies. The Syrian city of Palmyra is not only notable for the role it played in connecting networks in the Mediterranean and the Indian Ocean, but also on account of its rich epigraphic, iconographic and architectural record (Raja, 2022). The material from Palmyra reveals connections to the Mediterranean, to Mesopotamia, and to Syria as well as to the immediate surroundings of the Syrian Desert (Seland, 2016a). Long being discussed in terms of "western," "eastern" and "local," scholarship is now moving beyond this, in order to understand Palmyra in terms of different ways of expressing complex identities (Raja & Seland, 2024). Palmyrene self-representation is not only traceable in sculpture, architecture and epigraphy, but also reflected in the city plan, and thus a part of perceived space, that is firstspace.

Although there are obvious connections and parallels between funerary practice in Palmyra and elsewhere, the monuments, inscriptions and sculpture found in the *necropoleis* surrounding the ancient city are clearly directed toward the celebration of family and lineage (Gawlikowski, 1970; Henning, 2013, 2024). A telling sign of this is that virtually all of the large number of funerary inscriptions are in Aramaic. Sculptures in the funerary sphere include numerous portraits of women, not a common phenomenon in the admittedly much smaller record of public sculpture (Krag, 2018). The funerary sphere was not a place to communicate with outsiders. In contrast to, for instance, contemporary Roman cities like Pompeii and Ostia, where inscriptions celebrating the dead were often prominently placed for passers-by to see (Fig. 6.9).

Scholars have long debated the nature of the Palmyrene polity, was it a Mediterranean-style city state or an Arab-Aramaic tribal republic masquerading beneath a varnish of Roman-Hellenistic institutions (Ball, 1999; Sartre, 1996; Smith, 2004; Sommer, 2018)? If we visit the Agora the answer seems clear. Inscriptions abound, like we would expect in a Greek city, and they are often bilingual, but the longer version on top mostly in Greek (Delplace & Dentzer-Feydy, 2005). They mention city-state institutions such the council (*boule*) and the popular assembly (*demos*). This was a place for the Palmyrenes to celebrate their place in the world of city states.

Fig. 6.9 Funerary relief of Shalmat and Atenatan, mid-second century CE, Ny Carlsberg Glyptotek I.N. 1028 (*Photo* Eivind Heldaas Seland. CC BY-SA 4.0)

There are also other aspects of Palmyrene urban plan that connect the city with the Hellenistic *koinê* of the eastern Mediterranean. A prominent example is the theater. The construction of this monument started in the second or third century CE, and was never completed before the Roman sack of the city, 272 or 273 CE (Seigne, 2021, pp. 88–99). While there is little evidence of classical Greek dramatic tradition ever being popular in the Roman East, many cities constructed theaters in the Roman period. Segal suggests that performances would mostly consist of mimes, pantomimes and light entertainment (Segal, 1994, pp. 12–13). The buildings would also be suitable for any kind of public meetings. It has also been suggested that an unexcavated structure visible on aerial photographs might be an amphitheater (Hammad, 2008). These edifices, used for gladiatorial fights and animal spectacles are rare in the eastern provinces (Hammad, 2008; Pollard, 2000, p. 52), but relatively more common in the west, where they have been seen as a useful proxy for cultural Romanization (MacMullen, 2000). Blood sports were not as popular in the Roman East as in Italy and the west, and it is often assumed that amphitheaters were constructed for Roman garrisons or veterans, for which there is little evidence at Palmyra before the reign of Diocletian (284–385). Palmyra also boasted a Roman bath. The structure, misleadingly known as the Baths of Diocletian, was likely constructed between the rule of Hadrian (117–131) and the Severan dynasty (193–235) (Wielgosz, 2013). The investment in a major structure like this, dependent on water, heating and fuel, prominently situated on the main street of a desert city that had natural hot springs only a few hundred meters away, reveals a clear ambition to build a Roman city, where people could partake in distinctly Roman activities.

A different impression arises from the city's main sanctuary of Bel (Seyrig et al., 1975). The deity as well as the architectural plan has connections with Mesopotamia. Inscriptions are in Aramaic, Aramaic and Greek bilinguals, and also a few in Latin. Inscriptions frequently mention names of tribes, and some were made by outsiders. This was the largest and most prominent sanctuary of Palmyra, and Bel was at the center of Palmyrene pantheon. It seems that the temple was a place for the celebration of the Palmyrene commonwealth, which included not only the city, but also the nomads in the countryside and the diaspora-communities in Mesopotamia, Rome, Egypt and the Indian Ocean region.

Finally, the colonnaded street, constructed in the second and third centuries CE, picked up an architectural expression common all over the Roman Near East, but not elsewhere in the empire (Bührig, 2016; Burns, 2017). Inscriptions here celebrate Roman emperors, and the top figures of the Palmyrene elite, including the emerging royal dynasty that emerged in the mid-third century CE. These individuals were affiliated with imperial titles and honors, indicating that the monumental street is a part of the city suited for communicating Palmyra primarily as part of the Roman empire.

The example of Palmyra again underlines that space is different from place, in adding social and temporal dimensions to its spatial manifestation. Along with the sailing practices, texts and maps discussed above, the monuments of Palmyra allow us to go from firstspace, that is the perceived space that we can measure and experience as modern scholars for instance through GIS tools, and from secondspace or conceived space, meaning the representations of space contained in maps, texts or objects, to the thirdspace, lived space of the past or historical space. This is challenging, because our evidence is invariably limited, fragmentary, biased and subjective, and we depend on the interpretation of signs left from a past that we will never fully comprehend.

Approaching ancient long-distance connectivity through the lense of spatiality is nevertheless a way of moving from network to narrative and vice versa. The spatial dimension allows us to integrate the different networks of places, things, animals and people that have been discussed in the preceding chapters, and spaces actually also combine to constitute networks in their own right. If this appears vague, perhaps it is, but it is also a quite down to earth and concrete way of stating that scholars should aim not only to describe the past, but also to explain it.

Epilogue: Place, Space, Networks

The Alexandria described by Strabo at the turn of the Common Era, as cited at the outset of this book, was among the largest, most prosperous and well-connected cities of the ancient world. It had assumed this position already in the first generation after its foundation by Alexander the great (331 BCE), and it remained so for close to a millennium, even through the troubled period of the fifth and sixth centuries CE that saw religious strife, war, climatic turmoil and pandemic disease in the Roman world (Fowden, 2019).

This was to change in the seventh century CE. Sasanid occupation 619–28, Arab conquest 641 and several Byzantine attempts to retake the city up to 654 cut the city off from its Mediterranean hinterland. What had been the greatest commercial port and most important point of transit in the world became instead a frontier fortress and a naval depot. Coastal trade in the Mediterranean was largely replaced with overland caravans to Libya and Palestine, while the riches of the Nile no longer reached Alexandria, but were diverted by the renovated Nile-Red Sea canal toward the holy cities of Mecca and Medina. The erstwhile Roman fortress town of Babylon/al-Fustat took over the position at the intersection of commercial and political networks that Alexandria had once enjoyed, and would over time grow into the Medieval mega-city of Cairo (Fowden, 2019). As political and economic points of gravity changed, so did social networks. Greek merchants continued to be active in Egypt, the eastern Mediterranean and the Red Sea, but Jewish communities in India, South Arabia, Egypt and the Levant over time emerged as the dominant agents of transregional exchange in the Afro-Eurasian space along with Arab colleagues (Goitein & Friedman, 2008; Margariti, 2007; Power, 2012).

The changing fortunes of Alexandria highlight how cities depend on their networks. These are more often conceived of as hinterlands in urban geography, which emphasizes their natural resources and economic significance. But cities also engage with social, political and religious hinterlands. Approaching these in terms of networks rather than hinterlands makes it possible to avoid in-built notions about center and periphery and to engage also with how cities relate to each other.

As argued in this small book, cities are vital to our understanding of past connectivity and integration because they were the most prominent and stable nodes in the multidimensional networks that constituted the ancient world. We have traced the importance of geography and the natural environment for creating the basis and shaping the preconditions for exchange and connectivity (Chapter 2). In Chapter 3, we addressed the all-important role of human agents engaging in social networks in order to facilitate these processes. In Chapter 4, we approached the materiality of long-distance exchange, emphasizing not only the integrative role played by traveling objects, but also how they take on different social significance and fill different roles within different parts of a social network. Chapter 5 explored human-animal entanglement, and how ancient long-distance trade and mobility depended on the exploitation and cooperation of animals as commodities, carriers and even producers. Chapter 6 aimed to reconcile the spatial, social and temporal dimensions of ancient long-distance trade, by introducing spatiality as a heuristic tool to cross between them.

Afro-Eurasian connectivity was nothing new in the "Long Classical Millennium," c. 400 BCE–900 CE, and it did not come to an end in the subsequent period. Nevertheless, the period stands out as one of proto-global connectivity and integration. Many of the hallmarks of processes connected with globalization appear for the first time, including system-wide mobility of people, crops, animals and microorganism, along with exchange of ideas and innovations. Cities and the urban networks they formed were at the core of these processes, making them among the pivotal topics of interest in early history.

References

Abraham, S. A. (2023). Recent developments in the archaeology of long-distance connections across the ancient Indian Ocean. *Annual Review of Anthropology, 52*(1), 115–135.

Aḥmad ibn Majīd, al-S., & Tibbetts, G. R. (1971). Arab navigation in the Indian Ocean before the coming of the Portuguese: Introduction on the history of Arab navigation, notes on the navigational techniques and on the topography of the Indian Ocean. *Royal Asiatic Society of Great Britain and Ireland.*

Arnaud, P. (2005). *Les routes de la navigation antique: Itinéraires en Méditerranée*. Éditions Errance.

Ball, W. (1999). *Rome in the East: The transformation of an empire*. Routledge.

Beresford, J. (2013). *The ancient sailing season*. Brill.

Blue, L., Whitewright, J., & Thomas, R. (2011). 15: Ships and ships' fittings. In L. Blue & D. Peacock (Eds.), *Myos Hormos—Quseir al-Qadim. Roman and Islamic ports on the Red Sea. Volume 2: Finds from the excavations 1999–2003* (pp. 179–209). Archaeopress.

Bowersock, G. W. (2013). *Throne of Adulis: Red Sea wars on the eve of Islam*. Oxford University Press.

Brugge, R. B. (2017). To see or not to see: A study in maritime visibility. In Z. Tankosic, F. Mavridis, & M. Kosma (Eds.), *An island between two worlds: The archaeology of Euboea from prehistoric to Byzantine times: Proceedings of the International Conference, Eretria, 12–14 July 2013* (pp. 291–301). Norwegian Institute in Athens.

Bührig, C. (2016). The stage of Palmyra: Colonnaded streets, spaces for communication and activities in the eastern Roman Empire. In J. C. Meyer, E. H. Seland, & N. Anfinset (Eds.), *Palmyrena: City, hinterland and caravan trade between Orient and Occident* (pp. 59–76). Archaeopress.

Burns, R. (2017). *Origins of the colonnaded streets in the cities of the Roman East*. Oxford University Press.

Cappers, R. T. J. (2006). *Roman foodprints at Berenike: Archaeobotanical evidence of subsistence and trade in the Eastern Desert of Egypt*. University of California Los Angeles.

Carannante, A., Adam Woźniak, M., & Zych, I. (2022). More than just food from the sea: Exploitation of marine resources in Hellenistic Berenike on the Red Sea (Egypt). *Journal of Archaeological Science: Reports, 44*, Article 103515. https://doi.org/10.1016/j.jasrep.2022.103515

Casson, L. (1993). Ptolemy II and the hunting of African elephants. *Transactions of the American Philological Association, 123*, 247–260.

Casson, L. (1995). *Ships and seamanship in the ancient world*. John Hopkins University Press.

Cherian, P. J. (2016). (Ed.). *Pattanam excavations. Full reports 2007–2015*. Kerala Council for Historical Research.

Cobb, M. (2015). The chronology of Roman trade in the Indian Ocean from Augustus to early third century. *Journal of the Economic and Social History of the Orient, 58*(3), 362–418.

Cohen, G. M. (2006). *The Hellenistic settlements in Syria, the Red Sea Basin, and North Africa*. University of California Press.

Collar, A. (2017). Sinews of belief, anchors of devotion: The cult of Zeus Kasios in the Mediterranean. In H. F. Teigen & E. H. Seland (Eds.), *Sinews of*

Empire: Networks in the Roman Near East and beyond (pp. 23–36). Oxbow Books.

Dalché, P. G. (2007). The Reception of Ptolemy's Geography (end of the fourteenth to beginning of the sixteenth century). In D. Woodward (Ed.), *Cartography in the European Renaissance* (pp. 285–264). University of Chicago Press.

Delplace, C., & Dentzer-Feydy, J. (2005). *L'Agora de Palmyre*. Institut Ausonius / Institut français du Proche-Orient.

Facey, W. (2004). The Red Sea: The wind regime and location of ports. In P. Lunde, A. Porter, & S. Simpson (Eds.), *Trade and travel in the Red Sea region: Proceedings of the Red Sea project I* (pp. 7–17). Archaeopress.

Fauconnier, B. (2012). Graeco-Roman merchants in the Indian Ocean: Revealing a multicultural trade. *Topoi Suppl., 11*, 75–109.

Finley, M. I. (1973). *The ancient economy*. Chatto & Windus.

Fowden, G. (2019). Alexandria between antiquity and Islam: Commerce and concepts in first millennium Afro-Eurasia. *Millennium, 16*(1), 233–270.

Gawlikowski, M. (1970). *Monuments funéraires de Palmyre*. Warszawa: Editions scientifiques de Pologne.

Muthucumarana, R., Gaur, A. S., Chandraratne, W. M., Manders, M., Ramlingeswara Rao, B., Bhushan, R., Khedekar, V. D., & Dayananda, A. M. A. (2014). An early historic assemblage offshore of Godawaya, Sri Lanka: Evidence for early regional seafaring in South Asia. *Journal of Maritime Archaeology, 9*, 41–58.

Goitein, S. D., & Friedman, M. A. (2008). *India traders of the middle ages: Documents from the Cairo Geniza: India book*. Brill.

Hammad, M. (2008). Un amphithéâtre à Tadmor-Palmyre? *Syria, 85*, 339–346.

Henning, A. (2013). *Turmgräber von Palmyra*. Verlag Marie Leidorf.

Henning, A. (2024). Built for eternity. The funerary monuments of Palmyra. In R. Raja (Ed.), *The oxford handbook of palmyra* (pp. 365–380). Oxford University Press.

Horden, P., & Purcell, N. (2000). *The corrupting sea: A study of Mediterranean history*. Blackwell.

Hydrographer of the Navy. (1944). *Red Sea and Gulf of Aden Pilot* (5th ed.). Hydrographer of the Navy.

Kinda, A. (2017). Historical geography. In R. A. Marston, N. Castree, W. Liu, A. Kobayashi, M. F. Goodchild, & D. Richardson (Eds.), *The international encyclopedia of geography*. John Wiley & Sons, Ltd. https://doi.org/10.1002/9781118786352.wbieg0445

Kirwan, L. P. (1972). The Christian topography and the Kingdom of Aksum. *Geographical Journal, 138*, 166–177.

Kominko, M. (2013). *The world of Kosmas: Illustrated Byzantine codices of the Christian topography*. Cambridge University Press.

Krag, S. (2018). *Funerary representations of Palmyrene women*. Brepols.
Lane, F. C. (1963). The economic meaning of the invention of the compass. *The American Historical Review, 68*(3), 605–617.
Legg, S. (2025). Contesting monuments: Heritage and historical geographies of inequality, an introduction. *Journal of Historical Geography, 87*, 1–12.
MacMullen, R. (2000). *Romanization in the time of Augustus*. Yale University Press.
Marcotte, D. (2017). L'océan Indien des Grecs, entre tradition savante et actualité maritime. In E. Vagnon & É. Valet (Eds.), *La fabrique de l'océan Indien. Cartes d'Orient et d'Occident (Antiquité–XVIe siècle)* (pp. 31–40). Sorbonne.
Margariti, R. E. (2007). *Aden & the Indian Ocean trade: 150 years in the life of a medieval Arabian port*. University of North Carolina Press.
Massey, D. (2005). *For space*. Sage.
Metzler, D. (1989). Kaiserkult ausserhalb der Reichsgrenzen und römischer Fernhandel. In H.-J. Drexhage & J. Sünskes (Eds.), *Migratio et commutatio. Studien zur alten Geschichte und deren Nachleben. Thomas Pekáry zum 60. Geburtstag am 13. September 1989 dargebracht von Freunden, Kollegen und Schülern* (pp. 196–200). Scripta Mercaturae Verlag.
Ortelius, A. (1597). *(Xxxvi) Erythraei sive Rubri Maris Periplus*. Jan Baptista Vrients.
Parker, G. (2008). *The making of Roman India*. Cambridge University Press.
Peacock, D., Blue, L., Gebreyesus, Y., & Habtemichael, D. (2004). *The Eritreo-British Project at Adulis, interim report 2004*.
Pedersen, R. K. (2015). A preliminary report on a coastal and underwater survey in the area of Jeddah. *Saudi Arabia. American Journal of Archaeology, 119*(1), 125–136.
Pollard, N. (2000). *Soldiers, cities, and civilians in Roman Syria*. University of Michigan Press.
Power, T. (2012). *The Red Sea from Byzantium to the Caliphate: AD 500–1000*. American University of Cairo Press.
Radowska, J., & Zych, I. (2019). Exotic cults in Roman Berenike? An investigation into two temples in the harbour temenos. In A. Manzo, C. Zazzaro, & D. J. De Falco (Eds.), *Stories of globalisation: The Red Sea and the Persian Gulf from late prehistory to early modernity: Selected papers of Red Sea project VII* (pp. 225–245). Brill.
Ray, H. P. (2003). *The archaeology of seafaring in ancient South Asia*. Cambridge University Press.
Ray, H. P. (2006). Inscribed pots, emerging identities: The social milieu of trade. In P. Olivelle (Ed.), *Between the Empires: Society in India 300 BCE to 400 CE* (pp. 113–143). Oxford University Press.
Raja, R. (2022). *Pearl of the desert: A history of Palmyra*. Oxford University Press.

Raja, R., & Seland, E. H. (2024). Palmyra: At the crossroads of the ancient world. *Journal of Archaeological Research*. https://doi.org/10.1007/s10814-024-09203-8

Ramusio, G. B. (1550). *Navigationi et viaggi*. Stamperia de Giunti.

Rathmann, M. (2018). *Tabula Peutingeriana: Die einzige Weltkarte aus der Antike*. WBG, Philipp von Zabern.

Rougé, J. (1981). *Ships and fleets of the ancient Mediterranean*. Wesleyan University Press.

Sartre, M. (1996). Palmyre, cité grecque. *Annales Archéologiques Arabes Syriennes, 42*, 391–405.

Schulz, R. (2024). *To the ends of the earth: How ancient conquerors, explorers, scientists, and traders connected the world*. Oxford University Press.

Segal, A. (1994). *Theatres in Roman Palestine and Provincia Arabia*. Brill.

Seigne, J. (2021). *Observations sur la topographie de Palmyre*. Wydawnictwa Uniwersytetu Warszawskiego.

Seland, E. H. (2009). Shipwreck, maroons and monsters: The hazards of ancient Red Sea navigation. In L. Blue, J. Cooper, R. Thomas, & J. Whitewright (Eds.), *Connected hinterlands. Proceedings of the Red Sea project IV* (pp. 179–186). Archaeopress.

Seland, E. H. (2014). Archaeology of trade in the western Indian Ocean, 300 BC–AD 700. *Journal of Archaeological Research, 22*(4), 367–406.

Seland, E. H. (2016a). *Ships of the desert and ships of the sea: Palmyra in the world trade of the first three centuries CE*. Harrassowitz.

Seland, E. H. (2016b). Trade diasporas and merchant social cohesion in early trade in the western Indian Ocean. In D. H. Akenson & A. Chowdhury (Eds.), *Between dispersion and belonging: Global approaches to diaspora in practice* (pp. 125–137). McGill-Queen's University Press.

Seland, E. H. (2017). The archaeological record of Indian Ocean engagements in the Red Sea. In *Oxford handbooks online*. Oxford University Press. http://www.oxfordhandbooks.com/view/10.1093/oxfordhb/9780199935413.001.0001/oxfordhb-9780199935413-e-51

Seland, E. H. (2020a). Coastal and high-sea passages in ancient Red Sea navigation: Combining GIS with common-sense geography. In I. Mæhle, P. B. Ravnå, & E. H. Seland (Eds.), *Methods and models in ancient history: Studies in honor of Jørgen Christian Meyer* (pp. 99–110). Norwegian Institute at Athens.

Seland, E. H. (2020b). Red Sea studies: A historiographical sketch. *Polish Archaeology in the Mediterranean, 29*(1), 15–33.

Seland, E. H. (2022). Spaces, places and things. The spatial dimension of early Indian Ocean exchange. In F. Billé, S. Mehendale, & J. Lankton (Eds.), *The Maritime Silk Road. Global connectivities, regional nodes, localities* (pp. 27–42). Amsterdam University Press.

Seyrig, H., Amy, R., & Will, E. (1975). *Le temple de Bêl à Palmyre*. Librairie orientaliste Paul Geuthner.

Sidebotham, S. E. (2002). Late Roman Berenike. *Journal of the American Research Center in Egypt, 39*, 217–240.

Sidebotham, S. E. (2004). Reflections of ethnicity in the Red Sea commerce in antiquity: Evidence of trade goods, languages and religions from the excavations at Berenike. In P. Lunde & A. Porter (Eds.), *Trade and travel in the Red Sea region* (pp. 105–115). Archaeopress.

Sidebotham, S. E. (2008). Archaeological evidence for ships and harbor facilities at Berenike (Red Sea coast), Egypt. Memoirs of the American Academy in Rome. *Supplementary Volumes, 6*, 305–324.

Sidebotham, S. E. (2011). *Berenike and the ancient maritime spice route*. University of California Press.

Smith, A. M. I. (2004). Identity, community, and state formation at Roman Palmyra. In *Graduate School: Vol. Doctor of Philosophy*. University of Maryland.

Snyder, J. P. (2007). Map projections in the Renaissance. In D. Woodward (Ed.), *Cartography in the European Renaissance* (pp. 365–381). University of Chicago Press.

Soja, E. W. (1996). *Thirdspace: Journeys to Los Angeles and other real-and-imagined places*. Blackwell.

Sommer, M. (2018). *Roms orientalische Steppengrenze: Palmyra, Edessa, Dura-Europos, Hatra: Eine Kulturgeschichte von Pompeius bis Diocletian*. Franz Steiner.

Speidel, M. A. (2016). Die Throninschrift von Adulis und das Römische Reich am Roten Meer zu Beginn des dritten Jahrhunderts n. Chr. *Zeitschrift für Papyrologie und Epigraphik*, 287–300.

Strauch, I. (2012). *Foreign sailors on Socotra: The inscriptions and drawings from the Cave Hoq*. Hempen.

Talbert, R. J. A. (2010). *Rome's world: The Peutinger map reconsidered*. Cambridge University Press.

Thomas, R. (2012). Port communities and the Erythraean Sea trade. *British Museum Studies in Ancient Egypt and Sudan, 18*, 170–199.

Tomber, R. (2008). *Indo-Roman trade, from pots to pepper*. Duckworth.

Trombley, F. R. (2011). The imperial cult in late Roman religion (ca. AD 244–395): Observations on the epigraphy. In J. Hahn (Ed.), *Spätantiker Staat und religöser Konflikt. Imperiale und lokale Verwaltung und die Gewalt gegen Heiligtümer* (pp. 19–54). De Gruyter.

Warnking, P. (2015). *Der römische Seehandel in seiner Blütezeit: Rahmenbedingungen, Seerouten*. Verlag Marie Leidorf.

Weber, E. (1976). *Tabula Peutingeriana: Codex Vindobonensis 324: Vollständige Faksimile-Ausgabe im Originalformat*. Verlagsanstalt.

Wendrich, W. Z., Tomber, R. S., Sidebotham, S. E., Harrel, J. A., Cappers, R. T. J., & Bagnall, R. S. (2003). Berenike crossroads: The integration of information. *Journal of the Economic and Social History of the Orient, 46*(1), 46–87.

Whitewright, J. (2007). Roman rigging material from the Red Sea port of Myos Hormos. *International Journal of Nautical Archaeology, 36*(2), 282–292.

Wielgosz, D. (2013). Coepimus et lapide pingere: Marble decoration from the 'Baths of Diocletian' at Palmyra. *Studia Palmyreńskie, 13*, 319–332.

Zazzaro, C. (2013). *The ancient Red Sea port of Adulis and the Eritrean coastal region: Previous investigations and museum collections*. Archaeopress.

Zazzaro, C. (2017). Adulis and the sea. In D. A. Agius, E. Khalil, E. Scerri, & A. Williams (Eds.), *Human interaction with the environment in the Red Sea: Selected papers of Red Sea Project VI* (pp. 151–170). Brill.

Zazzaro, C., Cocca, E., & Manzo, A. (2014). Towards a chronology of the Eritrean Red Sea port of Adulis (1st—Early 7th century ad). *Journal of African Archaeology, 12*(1), 43–73.

Index

© The Editor(s) (if applicable) and The Author(s), under exclusive license to Springer Nature Switzerland AG 2026

E. H. Seland, *Long-Distance Trade in the Ancient World*, Palgrave Studies in Ancient Economies,
https://doi.org/10.1007/978-3-031-90855-2

9783031908545